C000134887

Welcome to Let's Go Carp Fishing and, whether you're after your first carp or your next carp this book will help you catch it.

If you've been carp fishing before then you will understand what makes it the most exciting form of angling there is. No freshwater fish fights like a carp and those of us that have been lucky enough to catch a few will never forget our first.

I spent a couple of years as a young boy cutting my angling teeth on the canals and rivers of Cheshire before I was finally invited to fish a local stillwater, where carp lived! I was 10 years old and, early one Sunday morning, I set off with just my next-door neighbour, my begged and borrowed tackle and my packed lunch for company – together, of course, with my dream of hooking a fish bigger than the usual roach and perch that occasionally hung themselves on my baited line!

I would like to say that my first carp fishing trip was a resounding success, but I'd be lying. My roach 'pole' was not up to the task in hand and I lost three giants. They were huge, and for weeks my tales of 'the three that got away' bored my friends and family to tears. I look back now and can only imagine the size of those leviathan carp – surely, at least three or four-pounders!

Some weeks later I had a birthday and my good behaviour over the previous year (ahem) was rewarded with some proper fishing tackle. A month later I made a repeat trip with my neighbour, landed my first-ever carp of 4lb 2oz and was hooked! I will never forget the heart-stopping moment when I saw that first carp – I can close my eyes and be there, on the banks of The Dingle, within seconds. But, do you know what really ignited my desire to catch carp? It wasn't that first fish on the bank, but the three that I had hooked and lost previously. To feel the power of those first fish and to have lost them without even seeing a single scale or fin sparked something inside me that will never leave me.

Wherever you live in the UK, and particularly in England, you are never far from a carp fishery, so get yourself out there and go catch some carp.

Marc Coulson

Editor

Name: Marc Coulson
Nickname: Pie Man
Age: 33
Occupation: Editor, Total Carp; group editor for all DHP carp titles
UK PB: 24lb 8oz

Assistant Editor

Name: Jon Bones
Nickname: Bonesy
Age: 21
Occupation: Deputy editor, Total Carp
UK PB: 36lb 8oz

Contents

Page 14

Page 24

Page 57

Page 42

Page 58

Page 60

Page 77

Page 98

Page 106

Rods & Reels

There are hundreds of carp rods on the market these days, each claiming to be able to outperform the next. However, there are certain characteristics that help separate these rods into categories, such as casting rods, short-range rods, stalking rods, floater fishing rods and so on.

The easiest way to choose which one to buy is to first work out what sort of fishing you are most likely to be doing. For example, if you are planning to fish a large pit and need to cast a long way, you'll need a rod of around 3lb to 3.5lb test curve. This will cope with the stresses of casting heavy leads a long way.

However, if you are only ever going to fish smaller waters for smaller fish, then you'll only need a light rod, say 2.25lb to 2.5lb test curve. This will give you a nice rod on which to experience the thrill of playing carp to the bank. If you are not sure, then opt for something like a 12 foot, 2.75lb test curve rod – suitable for most carp fishing situations.

You needn't pay a fortune for carp rods either; there are loads on the market now for very sensible money. For example, the excellent Chub Outkast rod, in a 2.75lb test curve, will only set you back around £60.

It's a similar tale with reels. Big-pit reels are designed for long casting, but a mid-sized model will more than suffice for the newcomer to carp fishing. One thing you should look out for is a free-spool facility, which allows fish to take line and so avoids your rod being pulled into the lake!

Great rods like this needn't break the bank.

Small reels like this Shakespeare model are a good starter option...

... before you progress to a big-pit reel, like this Daiwa Emcast.

Choose the right
rod-and-reel combination,
and casting becomes easy.

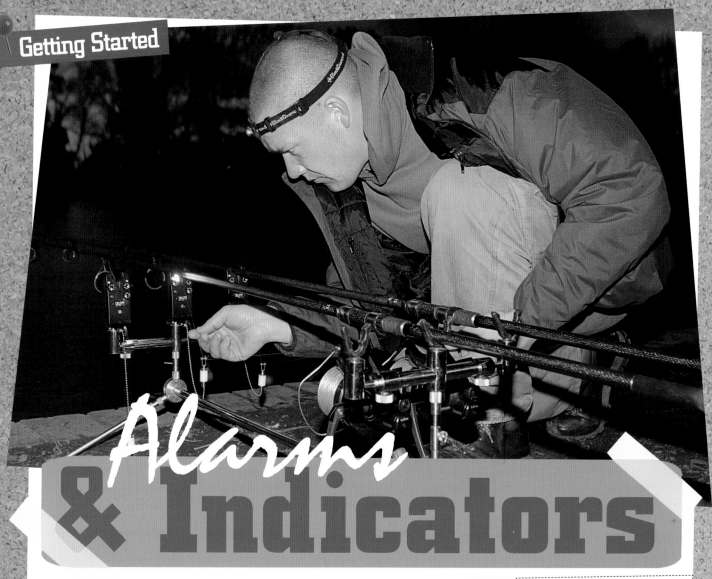

Alarms & Indicators

This lot costs less than £100.

While not essential, unless you're fishing at night, a set of alarms will make your life a lot easier. There are all-singing, all-dancing alarms with vibration settings, remote receivers and various other features as well as run-of-the-mill alarms. A set of top-end alarms will set you back a lot of money but, to be honest, to the average carp angler these alarms offer little more than a bog-standard one.

All you really need is an alarm that's reliable and has an on/off switch. Nowadays you can get an alarm like this for no more than a tenner. In fact, if you shop around you can now get three alarms and a receiver for less than £100.

To accompany the alarms you'll need a set of indicators. The choice is endless, but a simple bobbin or a swinger is a good starting point. Either of these two indicators will cover 99 per cent of the situations you'll find yourself in. As long as they're well made and won't fall apart as soon as you take them out of the packaging you'll be fine.

Finally you need something to put your alarms onto. If you fish a lot of venues that have hard banks or wooden platforms then a pod will be your best choice. As with most things the choice of pods is endless and prices vary dramatically. Your best bet is to shop around until you find one that's right for you. If the banks on your venue aren't rock hard then banksticks might be the choice for you.

These are more versatile than a pod, but obviously can't be used on platforms or solid ground. Although they can be quite expensive these will last you a lifetime.

Pods, great for venues with hard ground.

Strong banksticks will last a lifetime.

Oval brollies are fine for summer night sessions...

... but you'll want a bivvy for the winter nights.

Protection

Okay, first things first. You have to wear clothes to go fishing! No, we haven't suddenly gone mad. We all know that you cannot go carp fishing naked, but are there any special clothes you need?

Well no, not really, but it is very much in vogue to wear camouflage gear these days. 'Look good, feel good' is the motto of every fashion-conscious carp angler.

Realtree is the leading name in camou clobber, but other companies offer their own patterns too. Get yourself down to your local tackle shop and check some out for yourself. You can see how effective it can be in Undercover Carping on pages 71 to 76.

Clothing alone won't be enough to protect you from the elements when carp fishing. If you are only ever going to fish day sessions get an easy-erect day shelter. These go up in seconds and will offer protection from the wind and rain.

If you plan on doing a few overnight sessions in the summer, then you'll want something more like an oval brolly. With extended sides and all-round protection, this'll be fine for night fishing in warmer conditions.

However, if you fancy going the whole hog and fishing all year round, at night as well as in the day, you'll want a proper bivvy.

These offer fabulous protection from rain and even stronger winds, and are like a home from home for today's carp angler.

This style of shelter is great for day fishing.

Check out the camou gear that today's carpers wear!

Baits

R ather than go into detail about which baits to use in what situation, as this is covered in the bait chapter starting on page 36, these two pages are here to give you a starting point when selecting a bait. There are so many baits out there that choosing one to use can be an absolute nightmare.

Bait is one area where you shouldn't tighten the purse strings. Quality is of the utmost importance, so buy baits that are manufactured by reputable bait companies and always use the highest-quality bait you can afford.

Boilies

When selecting a boilie, go for one that's a proven carp catcher. You don't have to follow the latest trend, whatever that may be, just pick a bait that has an established track record. Stick to baits that are manufactured by reputable companies rather than opting for a cheaper alternative. It may cost you a pound or two more, but it'll definitely pay off in the long run.

If you only go fishing occasionally, or only use boilies as hook baits, then choose ready-made, shelf-life boilies. These can be kept in your rucksack and will last for ages. On the other hand, if you're planning on using boilies to bait up with, opt for freezer baits. These cost a little more than shelf-life baits and need to be kept in a freezer between sessions, but are far superior for baiting up with.

Pellets

Be careful when buying pellets, as not all varieties are allowed on some venues. Check the rules of your fishery before choosing your pellets because turning up with a bait that's banned will do you no good at all. Both trout and halibut pellets, which are dark in colour and very oily, are extremely good baits. They're readily available and cheap too, so if they're allowed on your venue then give them a try. Carp pellets, which are light in colour and have a lower oil content than trout pellets, are allowed on almost all venues. If trout and halibut pellets are banned on your venue then carp pellets are a great alternative.

Believe it or not, pellets do go off. You should only keep pellets for a couple of months before discarding any that are unused. You won't be able to tell just by looking at them, but the oil in the pellets will go rancid.

Unfortunately the quality of pellets varies massively, especially with things like hemp pellets, so be careful what you buy.

Don't just think of pellets as a loose feed. Large pellets make excellent hook baits and smaller pellets can be scalded with boiling water and made into a paste.

Liquids

Oils, glugs, dips and flavours are all great for boosting the attraction of your baits. Oil-based liquids can be used neat in PVA bags, which is a great winter method. Obviously, water-based liquids will melt the PVA.

Liquids are by no means a necessity and if you're on a budget then give them a miss, but they can give your baits an edge.

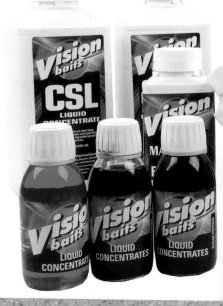

Pop-Ups

Pop-ups come in all the colours and flavours under the sun. You can get drawn into selecting a pop-up simply because it's new or you haven't seen it before, but don't. You are far better off sticking with proven baits that have stood the test of time, much the same as with the boilies. Bearing in mind that a tub of pop-ups will easily last for an entire season, you don't need more than a couple of tubs. If you're struggling with what to buy then three flavours you won't go far wrong with are; Pineapple, Tutti Frutti and Squid & Octopus. Pop-ups, like shelf-life boilies, won't go off and can be kept in your rucksack for absolutely ages.

Particles

'Particles' is a general term given to any bait that's a seed, a nut or a pulse. This includes hemp, tiger nuts, kidney beans, chick peas, maize and many others.

They are superb for baiting up with because carp love them and they're cheap. If bought unprepared in bulk you can get an awful lot of bait for less than £10. All particles need preparing before you use them. Using them unprepared can be dangerous to the fish. If you are unsure about how to prepare particles then buy them ready-prepared, such as those from Dynamite Baits.

Some venues have a particles ban, so make sure you're allowed to use them before doing so.

Just some of the essential carp fishing items.

Accessories

S o, we've covered all of the main items of tackle that you need to get started, but what about the little bits and bobs – the essentials?

Well, there are lots of other things that you'll need, the most important of which include a landing net, unhooking mat, luggage and, of course, a rod licence. If you plan on using more than two rods, you'll need to buy two licences.

If you are going to fish a lot in the summer then a pair of polarising sunglasses is a great addition. These special lenses reduce the glare on the water and so help you to see deep into the carp's world.

Things like bedchairs and sleeping bags are only necessary if you plan on doing lots of night fishing (see pages 98 to 101), but a decent chair will make even short sessions more comfortable.

Then there are all the rig bits known as terminal tackle, which include leads, hooks, rig materials and all manner of extra bits and pieces. These are essential for modern carp angling, but you needn't get carried away. For around fifty quid you can kit yourself out with the basic terminal tackle and then just progress from there. You'll soon build up a list of favourites as well as a collection of all manner of bits and pieces.

These modern leaders are well worth investing in.

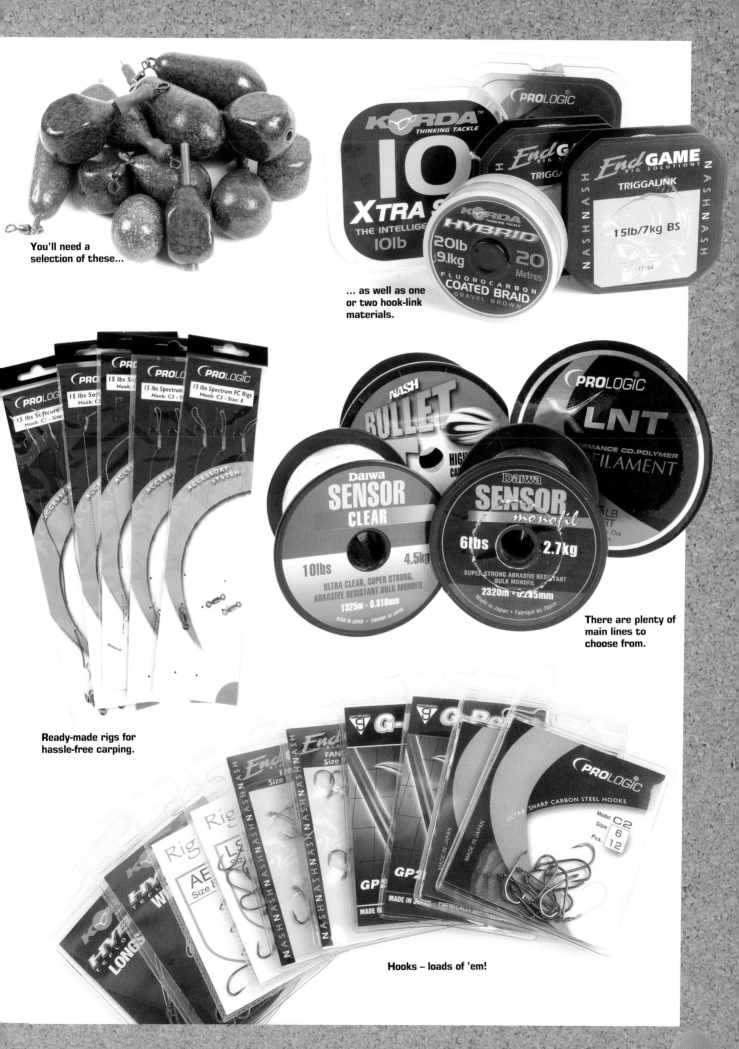

You'll need a selection of these...

... as well as one or two hook-link materials.

Ready-made rigs for hassle-free carping.

There are plenty of main lines to choose from.

Hooks – loads of 'em!

ANGLER FILE

Name: Simon Scott
Age: 35
UK PB: 52lb
Occupation: Course tutor
/college lecturer

A stunning 20lb-plus carp caught after identifying a feeding area.

Improve Your Watercraft

How do you find hotspots, like gravel bars and silty areas rich in natural food? Let's Go Carp Fishing asks Simon Scott to explain...

Simon Scott is one of the best anglers in the country at identifying where carp are in a lake. He's also very good at knowing exactly where to place his hook baits.

With this in mind, we decided to interview him on his location skills in an attempt to find out just why it is Simon catches the number of big fish that he does. After all, anyone who catches 39 fish from the awesome Wraysbury over three years (including nearly all the big fish) has to be a very talented angler!

We decided to begin the interview with the absolute basics, and asked Simon briefly to explain what plumbing is – and how useful it can be to the modern carp angler.

SS: Plumbing is the term used to describe the process of depth and feature finding. It's done using a heavy lead of 3oz or 4oz and a buoyant, easily visible float (called a marker float). Some anglers will often use a braided main line as well, for extra sensitivity.

I would say that plumbing is a vital skill that the modern carp angler should learn. When done accurately, it's the best way of finding out the depth of the swim you are fishing and gauging the topography of the lake bed (unless you have access to a boat and echo sounder).

However, it's also important to learn when to plumb. If you arrive at your lake to find fish head-and-shouldering in a localised area, you should NOT start chucking in a 4oz lead and bright orange float over their heads. In situations like this it's far better to cast out two or three single hook baits rather than a marker float.

Don't become a slave to plumbing. Learn to recognise the situations where it would be beneficial. Too many times I see anglers turn up in a swim and then ruin their chances by thrashing the water to a foam with a plumbing rod.

LGCF: So when do you plumb, and why?

SS: I plumb mostly when I'm researching a venue prior to fishing, or prior to a season-long campaign. Generally I like to know the lake reasonably well before I actually fish it.

I do use marker floats when fishing – for example, on well-stocked waters, or when I know I stand very little chance of catching anything.

I used a marker float at Old Bury Hill during a night fishing session in the autumn. At places like Bury Hill, which are crammed with carp, I'll use a marker float as a target to help me bait an area I think the fish will pass through. This will ensure accurate baiting and casting. It will also help me locate features on the lake bed that I think will hold carp.

> SOME FEATURES CAN ONLY BE FOUND WITH THE SKILLED USE OF A MARKER FLOAT.

Indeed, it's for locating underwater features, depth and also determining the type of bottom I have in front of me that I find plumbing set-ups and marker floats most useful.

At Old Bury Hill I used the float to find a small gulley in open water, which I then baited up, cast to and caught from. Without the float I would not have been able to do that, but I kept the use of the float to a minimum so it wouldn't spook too many fish.

LGCF: What sort of underwater features are you looking for? What makes them so attractive to carp?

SS: I'm looking for changes in depth. I'm also looking to feel what the lake bed is made from.

More specifically, on gravel pits I'd be looking

How To Tie Simon's Plumbing Rig

1 Simon now uses indestructible Wychwood markers. The other marker he is holding broke after excessive use!

2 Si uses braided main line. It has no stretch and transmits what the lake bed feels like to him as he plumbs.

3 The lead is attached to a Wychwood plumbing link, which has a cork attached to one end for buoyancy.

4 The other end of the plumbing link has a clip on it, so you can change leads quickly and easily.

5 The links are stiff, which means they stick up above weed and silt, allowing your float to rise to the surface.

6 Here are the two leads Simon uses when plumbing. The lead on the left is a Wychwood Grubber.

7 Thread your main line through the link, then tie on your marker with another cork below. This improves buoyancy.

8 Select which lead you want to use and place it on the clip. When plumbing a new swim, Si uses smooth leads.

9 The finished marker rig. This is how it should work when dragged across the lake bed – essential for feature finding.

for gravel bars, plateaux, gravel ridges and silty areas. These can all be excellent features to fish to, and are features that can only be found with the skilled use of a marker float as they are usually invisible from the bank.

I like to find out where these features are in the lake. I also try and map what direction any gravel bars run in, how large they are and how big the stones are that the bars are made from.

People often ask me why gravel bars produce so many fish. I think the answer is that they form part of the route that a carp will follow as it swims around a lake, a bit like an underwater road. It could be that carp use bars to navigate their way around lakes.

Anglers should remember that any underwater feature that's distinctive, given its surroundings, may regularly be visited by patrolling carp.

LGCF: But not all lakes are gravel pits. Does the same theory about features apply to smaller lakes and ponds that weren't dug for gravel extraction?

SS: Broadly speaking, yes. In seemingly flat-bottomed silty lakes, a feature that attracts carp could prove to be a slightly raised hard patch or a sandy ridge a foot or two across.

Even more amazingly, if you can find a depth difference that's just a couple of inches deeper or shallower than the norm you could be onto a winner. On a lake bed that's as flat as a pancake, a gulley or a hole that's barely detectable by a marker float could end up producing fish. But you need to plumb hard when not fishing and watch the carp for clues as to where such areas might be.

As I said, the key is this; any underwater feature that is distinctive, given its surroundings, may regularly be visited by patrolling fish.

LGCF: Can you give examples of the types of features you are talking about?

Simon doesn't plumb all the time – if he finds feeding fish, he'll cast to them without plumbing up first.

SS: Yes. Firstly I'll give you an example of a feature I found once on the bottom of a small, seemingly featureless lake that was quite silty.

The lake in question happened to be the birthplace of modern carp fishing, Redmire. I was privileged enough to fish there a few years ago and caught several carp to just over 20lb from a small hole I located in the silt.

I found the hole by watching the carp and seeing if I could identify their patrol routes. Within a few hours I'd done this and soon noticed that, time and again, the fish would keep visiting one small area – an area which was right on a major patrol route in open water.

In an opportune moment I decided I had to find out why the fish were so interested in that spot, so I gently lobbed a marker float out and did a quick bit of plumbing. I discovered that the lake bed there was a few centimetres deeper than its surroundings.

The hole could have been created by carp feeding on a bloodworm bed. I don't know why they loved it so much, but there's no doubt that the depth variation – no matter how small it was – was important.

At the other end of the scale, at Wraysbury, where I have been fishing over the last three summers, there's a well-known hotspot about 40 yards out from a swim known as 'Mary's Point'.

The feature in question cannot be seen from the bank, but when you look at it from a boat through a glass-bottomed bucket you can see that it's simply awesome. It comprises a huge gravel bar that rises out of 14 feet of water – with the top of the bar being seven feet down from the surface.

The bar is known as 'Mary's Table' and is

Three Top Tips! The Easy Way To Plumb

1

With your plumbing rod rigged up, get into a swim and cast out into open water to see what the topography of the lake bed is like.

2

After they have sunk, start pulling the lead and float slowly back towards you, feeling what the lake bed is like along the way.

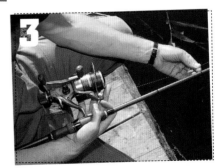

3

When you find an area where gravel meets silt, pop the float up a foot at a time to gauge depth and mark the spot.

Which Bottom Should I Fish Over?

Lake Bed One
Bars made up of large stones aren't usually productive. Carp can't feed as effectively over stones this size.

Lake Bed Two
Bars made from smaller gravel pieces like this are far better. Carp can extract natural food from such stones.

Lake Bed Three
Brown, non-smelly silt is Simon's favourite lake bed. It harbours nutritious bloodworm and other goodies.

approximately 15 feet long by four feet wide. The sides of the bars are sheer drop-offs that resemble mini cliffs. Yet a bait placed on top of the bar caught Wraysbury's most famous resident, Mary the mirror, on a few occasions.

LGCF: Why did fish get caught from this feature?

SS: I don't precisely know why it was such a favourite area for the carp. Perhaps it was because the bar is located in such a position that carp travelling back and forth from the north and south lakes of Wraysbury often track across the top of it. Therefore, when anglers put bait on it, they would drop down and feed from time to time.

Certainly a hook bait placed on 'Mary's Table' stood a reasonable chance of being taken if the fish were in the right mood.

LGCF: We've learned so far that good location relies a lot on watching the water and noting patrol routes of carp. When you find these routes, you then need a marker float to plumb and find an underwater feature on the lake bed that the carp might like feeding on or around. What sort of plumbing set-up do you use, and why do you use it?

SS: I use Wychwood Grubber Leads quite a lot, along with Wychwood marker floats.

Grubber leads are fantastic for gaining sensitive information from the lake bed. They are also great at bringing back samples of debris from the bottom of the lake, so you can establish what you're fishing over.

However, when I start plumbing on a new lake I will use a plain lead with my plumbing set-up. Plain leads drag across the bottom more easily and are ideal for feature finding when you don't really know what kind of features are in front of you.

When you have some idea what the lake bed

Simon demonstrates that Wychwood markers are indeed indestructible.

Plumbing – a skill all carp anglers should learn.

comprises of, switch to a Grubber Lead to check out really localised spots intimately.

The Wychwood floats are the best marker floats I have used. They are buoyant and robust. In fact, they are virtually indestructible (which is just as well because I have a habit of destroying just about all the marker floats I ever use).

I sometimes cut a Wychwood float in half for plumbing in small-water situations and where it isn't too weedy. These create less disturbance than huge marker floats.

LGCF: When using your plumbing set-up, what sort of lake bed would you ideally like to find? Are gravel bars and gravelly features really the best areas to catch carp?

SS: Not necessarily. The productivity of gravel areas depends on the time of year, the water temperature and the kind of gravel the bar is made from. Also, it depends on whether the spot

you've found has received a lot of pressure from anglers in preceding months.

In a lightly fished venue, a gravel plateau may be a great spot to intercept fish. But be aware that, when they have been caught a few times, they might avoid feeding on that plateau again.

It might seem strange, but the type of gravel you are fishing over is important too. I remember Dave Lane saying how he found that bars made from big stones at Wraysbury were less productive than bars made from small stones.

There's something in this. I reckon it could be because carp find it easier to find food among small stones. Think of how carp feed. The kind of natural feed you find in such an environment – shrimp, hoglouse, caddis and snails – are far easier to root out among small stones. Carp can actually pick up smaller-sized gravel particles and blow them out after separating and swallowing food items among them.

LGCF: Does small gravel hold a lot of natural food? And whereabouts on gravel bars should you cast - the top of the bar, the slope or the base?

SS: Gravel holds different types of natural food, but probably not as much as fertile silty areas. In silt you are more likely to find bloodworm, which at certain times of the year – especially in the autumn and winter – carp definitely seem to prefer eating.

Bloodworm offers the carp masses of nutrition. When bloodworm are 'ripe' they represent a huge source of food. So if you find an area of silt when plumbing, and you happen to be bringing the odd bloodworm back on your Grubber lead, you have probably found a great area to fish.

I am a big fan of silty areas and have caught a lot of fish from them. Therefore, if I had the choice when fishing a gravel bar, I would cast a hook bait to the base of the bar where the gravel meets the silt.

Also, I prefer fishing over silt because I'm sure carp find it harder to differentiate between freebies and the hook bait when feeding over it.

What Natural Carp Food Should I Look For?

If you can find silty areas near gravel bars that hold bloodworm like this, you're onto a winner!

Snails live in weed and gravel. Areas where there are snails will have carp nearby.

These are hoglouse. They live around stones, the bases of bars and in certain weeds.

These are freshwater shrimp. Usually found in weed and small stones, carp love them.

Believe it or not, there is a caddis nymph in this case. Found mainly on gravelly bottoms.

Weed that contains plenty of natural food indicates areas that are well worth investigating.

For a carp, feeding over a polished gravel area must be like feeding on a clean table. It must be far easier for it to identify a hook bait presented here than a hook bait presented over silt.

When feeding over silt, carp have to do far more 'processing' of each mouthful before they can find and swallow any food items. In my opinion this means they are more likely to move away with your rig in their mouth – and therefore more likely to hook themselves than they would if they were feeding over a clean lake bed.

LGCF: Are some types of silt better to fish in than others? How do you find the

'right type of silt' to fish over?

SS: Not all silt contains nutritious food like bloodworm and hoglouse. Naturals do not like smelly, anoxic silt (anoxic silt is silt that doesn't contain much dissolved oxygen).

This type of silt, which tends to be jet-black and stinks, is created by rotting organic matter such as leaf debris. It really is not worth fishing over. Dark-brown silt, that doesn't smell, is far more likely to be favoured by bloodworm. That, in turn, means carp are more likely to feed over it.

If you're you're struggling to find 'good silt' I'd suggest finding an area where gravel borders silt. You can find this type of area easily enough when plumbing. Any area where gravel rises from silt could be good.

If you can find any areas with this sort of make up, you'll be in with a chance of catching.

If you can find such a spot where you've also seen a few carp, even better. If a patrol route is nearby you might just have hit the location jackpot!

If permitted, Simon wades around lakes examining the lake bed for clues as to where the carp might feed.

Chop your marker float in half if you don't want to spook fish so easily.

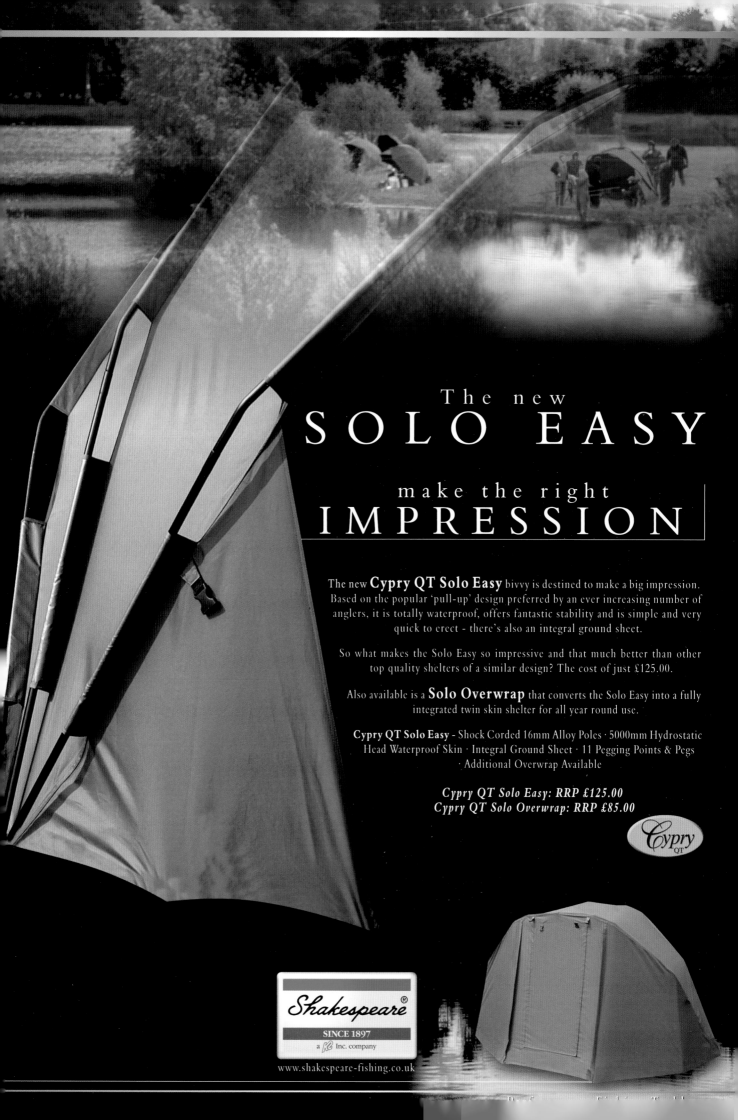

Location Location Location

In the right situation a marker float can aid location. But don't overuse it.

Marc Coulson starts you off with his guide to fishing in the right areas.

Choosing the right location to fish is largely down to your watercraft. So, what exactly is this thing that so many carp anglers refer to all the time? Well, it's more important than any rig, tackle or bait that you'll ever use and it's also something that you learn more of with experience.

Neither I, nor anyone else for that matter, can just give you the skill of watercraft, but I can at least start you on the right road. Watercraft is, in a nutshell, understanding the water in front of you and being able to increase your chances of finding carp by reading the signals from it.

That's a far from definitive description of watercraft, but it pretty much covers what it is all about. So, what are the signs that you should look for and how many factors should you take into consideration when looking for carp in your chosen water? Here are a few to get you started…

Carp love cover in the margins.

Learn to read the wind direction.

Islands

How many times have you turned up at a water and thought: "I'll fish to that island, there are bound to be carp there."? I have lost count of the waters I have been to where the swims that give access to islands are the most worn ones.

Yes, islands are a great starting point, but you should give them a little more thought. Points of islands, overhanging trees and bushes and small bays in the islands are always worth closer inspection.

If you can cast well, go for the side of the island that requires the longest chuck. Many anglers will not be able to reach these points and so the carp may often feel safe in these areas. The side that requires the shortest cast will always receive lots of pressure.

Margins

Too many anglers set up and cast out as far as they can. Don't ignore the margins. Look for signs close in of possible carp movement. Movement in nearside reeds and lily pads will almost always mean that there are carp in there – unless they are followed by the scampering of a coot or such like!

A slight rocking of the water or possibly even swirls will betray the presence of carp. Cloudy areas of water will often signal that a carp has fed on the bottom there recently – it may still be there or at least will probably return. Little plumes of oil and small slicks on the surface will again often give the carp's presence away. Look for all of these little things and get used to recognising them as signs of carp activity.

Wind Direction & Weather

Always make a note of the wind direction and try and keep a record of the prevailing winds on any water that you visit regularly. A good general rule is to follow the wind if it is mild and to fish the back of the wind when it is cold.

However, these are just starting points and there are always exceptions to every such rule. Make a note of fish sightings or captures in different conditions and you will soon see patterns emerging.

Don't Be Lazy

Ask yourself the golden question: "If I was a carp, where would I be right now?" The chances are you would go to the area that is receiving the least pressure – often the furthest spots from the car park! Don't be lazy – get yourself round there and have a look.

Birdlife

Watch the waterfowl on the lake. See where they are diving and watch their patrol routes. If you have nothing else at all to go on, then I wouldn't mind betting that the carp will have similar patrol routes. They feed on many of the same things as the ducks and coots so might just be in the same areas.

Stay Alert

NEVER take your eyes off the water for longer than you have to. I have seen fish show themselves on many occasions when I know that the other anglers have not, because they are not watching the water.

I have even wound in and recast my rods to showing fish without anyone else being any the wiser. This is a great way of catching a few bonus fish.

Always watch the water.

Think Differently

Don't just sling your marker float out and look for gravel. I have caught infinitely more carp from silt and the edge of weed beds than I ever have off gravel. Give your marker float work some thought. Don't be too hasty in over-using the marker either – it can be the biggest carp scarer around and I only ever use mine if I have absolutely nothing else to go on. This is less than 10 per cent of the time, I might add.

Be Observant

In a similar way to watching the water for crashing fish, look also for flat spots and other slight changes in the surface of the lake. A flat spot can often give away the presence of a carp just under the surface and can also mean that there is oily bait on the bottom that is being disturbed. These are more vital signs that you should learn to recognise.

Keep A Log

My absolute number one tip to everybody, wherever and however you're fishing, would be to keep a record of everything that you catch, where you catch it and how. These records can be absolutely vital in maintaining your success rate. They also help build up your understanding of the relationship between carp and conditions, your lake and all manner of factors.

Try casting close to marginal snags.

Worn swims often mean pressured areas – try elsewhere.

When fishing to islands, choose the less-pressured side.

SIMON DAVEY
+ HYDROLINK
= THORPE PARK
COMMON

Rig Marole
FINELY TUNED TACKLE

www.rigmarole.co.uk

Mastermind

Dave Lane, one of the country's best carp anglers, answers questions on all things carpy.

Q Which winds are best for fishing and do the carp hide in a particular place in relation to the wind?

A There are five major airflows that affect Britain, basically one from each direction apart from west, which has two totally different systems. Northwesterlies bring polar air, while southwesterlies bring tropical airflows. Winds from the arctic north and polar east both bring cold air and the tropical winds from the south and southwest will bring warmer air currents.

On Diagram 2 you can see that two different airflows, NE and NW, will have almost the same effect on the water by blowing into the shallows. Fish will follow both winds in the summer but during winter the northwesterly will almost certainly be more productive in this area. On the northeast wind, which is colder, the fish may well move onto the back of it into.

Fish have a high level of sensitivity to air (or water) pressure and will always know what weather is on its way. It is not uncommon for the carp to pre-empt the weather and be sat on the windward bank before the wind changes.

New winds will push the surface of the lake in one direction and, depending on depth and features on the lake bed, there will be an equal amount of water moving in the other direction below the surface. The effect of the undertow will depend on the depth of the lake, the angle of the windward bank and the strength of the wind (see Diagrams 1 and 3).

The undertow created by this water movement will eventually draw any food particles away from the windward bank.

Bear in mind that the wind will affect lakes in different ways depending on the lake's features

Basically, I would always fish on a new wind but be wary of becoming a slave to the wind direction, especially when the wind becomes 'stale' after a couple of days.

ANGLER FILE

Name: Dave Lane
Age: 43
Occupation: Product development manager, JRC
UK PB: 55lb

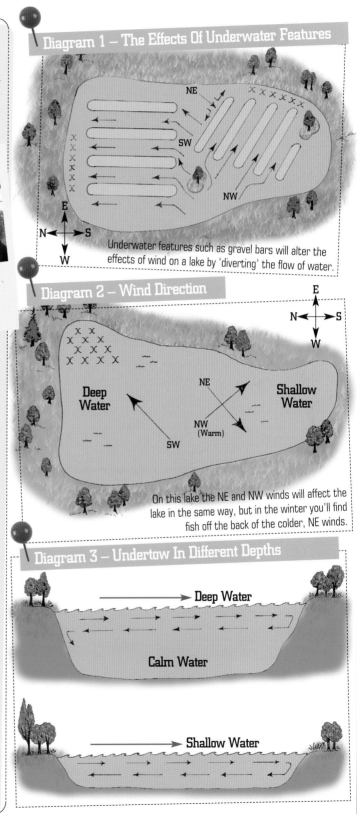

Diagram 1 – The Effects Of Underwater Features

Underwater features such as gravel bars will alter the effects of wind on a lake by 'diverting' the flow of water.

Diagram 2 – Wind Direction

Deep Water

Shallow Water

NE

NW (Warm)

SW

On this lake the NE and NW winds will affect the lake in the same way, but in the winter you'll find fish off the back of the colder, NE winds.

Diagram 3 – Undertow In Different Depths

Deep Water

Calm Water

Shallow Water

Key To Diagrams

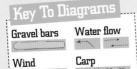

Gravel bars   Water flow

Wind   Carp

Rig Zone

Frank Warwick takes Marc Coulson into his confidence and reveals some of the rig secrets behind his amazing carp fishing success...

ANGLER FILE

Name: Frank Warwick
Age: 45
UKPB: 43lb 14oz
Nickname: Seventies porn star!
Favourite water: Hardwick, Linear Fisheries

Frank Warwick has caught more carp than many of us could ever dream of, both here and abroad. He has risen to 'celebrity' angler status and is now one of the most-recognisable faces on the circuit, drawing crowds from far and wide to meet him at the various shows.

His success is down to a number of factors, including his meticulous approach to rigs and presentations.

So, what rigs does Frank employ and does it matter? What else does he do with his presentations that might help readers put a few more fish on the bank?

I caught up with him at Roman Lakes in Cheshire and asked him to show me three things that readers can try for themselves. The results were very interesting.

The first thing that we talked about was the method by which Frank attached his hook baits. There is rarely any sign of a baiting needle; instead he ties his baits on using a grinner loop as a lasso. This might sound a bit odd to one or two of you, but have a look at our step-by-step guide and then think about how it could benefit you.

Don't Pierce Your Baits, Try This...

1

Take a decent length of your chosen coated hooklength. Strip back nine inches of the coating.

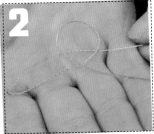

2

Double back the uncoated braid and then form a loop in one of the tags, like this.

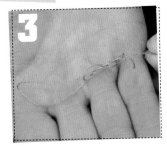

3

Pass the tag end through the loop and hook link, like so. Make at least five turns.

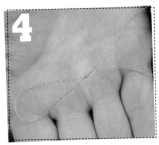

4

Tighten the whippings and loop down to form a sliding loop. Hang on, you're not done yet!

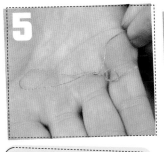

5

Tie a small overhand knot, or granny knot, in the tag end behind the loop.

6

Butt the granny knot down tight behind the loop knot. This stops it slipping. Now trim the tag end.

7

By pulling the hook link you can tighten the loop down. Trap your bait carefully and tighten fully.

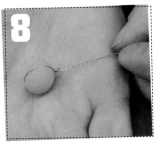

8

There you go - no need for piercing baits any more. You can change your bait easily too.

I asked Frank why he favours this way of tying his hook baits.

"I tell you mate, it's pretty simple really. By piercing your hook baits, you weaken the bait itself and can, in the case of pop-ups, lessen their effectiveness.

"A pierced pop-up will take on water and this can have a detrimental effect on its buoyancy. By tying the bait on there is no water penetration, except through the outside of the bait, as is the norm.

"The reason I use the sliding grinner loop is that it is extremely versatile. There is no fiddling about with tying small hair loops and it also eliminates the need for hair stops.

"I can change my hook bait in seconds and without fuss. I can also change the type of hook bait and size. If I am using a 15mm bait and decide that I need a bigger one, for example when there are nuisance fish about, I can slide the loop open and then insert the bigger bait. You know it makes sense!"

Frank added that it is not always possible to use the sliding grinner loop and pointed out that it's best used with braid or stripped-back coated braid, and not with monofilaments, as they can slip.

Take time to make sure your rigs are perfect.

Ready for action.

Getting your bite indication right is vital.

So, having established that the sliding grinner loop can be used to make bait attachment easy and adaptable, what sort of rig does Frank actually use it on? I asked him to show me the rig he would use if only allowed one:

"I'd have to use this one," he says, as he produces what looks like a combi rig with a very bright, orange bait attached.

"It's a pretty simple combi rig, such as you might often see in many of the magazines. I will add, however, how important it is to use components that you are confident in. I am a huge fan of long-shanked hooks and use the ones from Korda. I just like the way the hooks behave and I have every confidence in them. I will add here that I do not use long-shanked hooks inside a PVA bag. My rig changes to a short braid link with a Korda Wide Gape. I cannot quite put my finger on why, but I just don't think that long-shanked hooks work well in bags. The Wide Gape seems to outperform the long shank every time.

"Back to my standard rig, I also use a slight variation on a common theme, just to make the rig a bit safer and even more effective.

Frank Warwick's Rig To Take Anywhere

1 Once your bait is attached, tie a simple knotless knot, using a Korda Longshank.

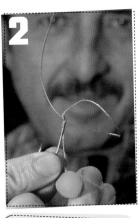

2 Now take the tag end back through the back of the hook's eye a second time.

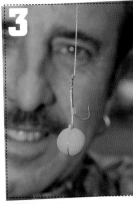

3 "This 'twice through the eye' knotless knot is twice as strong," says Frank.

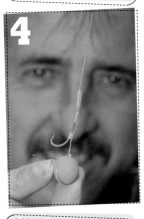

4 Add two short pieces of shrink tubing as shown here. Don't shrink it down yet.

5 Using a needle, thread the hook link through the front of the shrink tubing.

6 This forms a line aligner rig. You can steam the shrink tubing down now.

7 Frank adds a trimmed-down Korda shockleader sleeve to his hooklength.

8 He then ties on a swivel, using a grinner knot, to the end of the hook link.

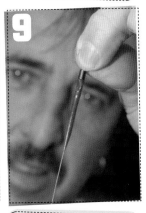

9 The sleeve then sits on the swivel like this, creating a nice anti-tangle boom.

> ## "HAVE YOU NEVER HEARD OF THE DROP-OFF INLINE SET-UP MATE?" FRANK ASKS ME.

"The first difference is that, when tying the knotless knot, I take the hook link back through the back of the eye TWICE when finishing off the knot. This adds a bit of strength to the knot and stops it ever slipping. This might never happen anyway, but it might, so it gives me more confidence in the rig.

"The second thing I do is combine the 'bent-hook effect' of using shaped shrink tubing with a line-aligner arrangement. Most people do one or the other, but I have not seen so many using both.

"Once the shrink tubing has been steamed down to form the bend, I use a needle to thread the hook link out through the front of it, making the rig even more effective.

Solid proof that Frank knows what he's talking about.

The 'Drop-The-Lead', Inline-Lead System

Frank has this great inline-lead system, perfect for fishing in weed or near snags.

To tie this lead system, start by tying a braid hook link and adding a size 8 swivel to it.

Push the swivel into the bottom of a Korda inline flat pear lead with the plastic insert in it.

Make sure that the swivel sits snugly inside the plastic insert, as Frank has done here.

Thread a Korda tail rubber onto the hook link and pull it down to the lead.

Push the tail rubber onto the plastic insert at the top of the lead, trapping the line in place.

As soon as the lead hits an obstacle, and often even on the take, it will shed the swivel...

... before dropping out of the tail rubber and falling off, allowing you to land the fish safely.

"I use a second piece of shrink tubing to make sure that the hair sits correctly. This also acts to position the bait in the best place to increase the hooking potential of the rig."

As we talk a bit more about rigs in general, I pick Frank's brains about fishing in weed and PVA bags. He has already explained that he uses a short braid rig inside PVA bags, and he tells me that an inline lead is normally best.

I fish a lake that is very weedy and I am concerned that inline leads can get caught up in the weed when I am playing a fish, so I ask Frank for his advice. He came up with an absolute gem and I had to get some pictures so that I could share it with you all.

"You're right about not wanting to use inline leads in weed or near snags. This is from both a fish-safety point of view and their effectiveness when playing and landing the carp.

"Have you never heard of the drop-off inline set-up mate?" Frank asks me.

"Obviously not," comes my reply.

"Right, here you go, try this one out..." he continues.

Frank then shows me a lead arrangement that allows the use of an inline lead, but also allows the lead to come off the rig should it become snagged. This will allow me to use the inline set-up when fishing my weedy water.

An effective rig will put carp on the bank!

Frank's rigs have accounted for some huge carp.

"By tying one end of a size 8 swivel along the hook link, you can then push it into the inline lead, leaving the hook link hanging out. The tag end is then passed through a tail rubber. Then, the tail rubber is attached to the lead, as per normal. This leaves the hook link coming through the tail rubber but not through the lead. The fact that the rig is fished inside a bag means that the force of the cast is absorbed and the rig remains intact.

"If a fish is hooked and charges off through the weed, the swivel comes out of the lead and the lead is then only held in place by the tail rubber. This requires hardly any pressure to pull off, so the lead drops away. Bingo!"

Try it next time you want to fish an inline lead but there's too much weed.

Smile. The hard part's over.

ANGLER FILE

Name: Steve Fantauzzi
Age: 30
UK PB: 37lb 12oz
Occupation: Fishing sales,
Yateley Angling Centre

Carp Care Masterclass

Tip One
Unhooking Mats – Which One?

Steve Fantauzzi passes on some essential tips that will ensure the carp you catch are well looked after when they're on the bank.

Have you ever caught a carp with a split fin or a couple of scales missing? Have you ever banked a fish that had a slightly dodgy mouth? The chances are that, at some stage, you have. If you haven't, I can almost guarantee that one day you will .

This is because carp angling is more popular than ever before. It's the fastest-growing sector of sportfishing in the UK. Kids coming into angling are getting straight into carp, rather than serving angling apprenticeships fishing for smaller species like roach, bream and tench. Therefore carp fisheries, especially day ticket lakes, are receiving more and more pressure – and the carp in them are being

caught more frequently than ever before. All of this means it's more essential than ever that us carp anglers get our act together and make sure that we treat the fish we catch with the respect they deserve. Captured carp must be put back in the water none the worse for their experience.

I have put together a number of tips that are designed to help you understand how you can care for the fish you catch. Whether you are a novice angler or are more experienced, there should be something here that will get you thinking and hopefully improve the way you treat your carp.

One of the most important items of kit any carp angler can possess is an unhooking mat. You should never go fishing without one, and every carp you catch should be placed on one when you come to unhook it. It doesn't matter how big the carp is when you catch it; treat it with the respect it deserves.

These days, unhooking mats don't cost much. I own two mats, a cheap Wychwood model that I use for stalking and a more expensive Nix Angling mat that I use when I'm fishing in one swim.

The Wychwood mat cost me £9.99 and offers a good degree of protection. It's large enough to cushion a fish over 30lb and is well padded. Everyone should be able to afford a mat of this standard, at the very least.

My other mat is a Nix Angling job. It costs just under £60, but it's very large, perfect for big fish, and extremely well padded.

Tip Two
Which Net?

It really annoys me when I see match and pleasure anglers with really small landing nets attempting to get big double-figure fish into them. When they do eventually succeed, the fish is usually hoisted out of the water while doubled over. Sometimes all the weight of the captured carp rests on its tail, or on a pectoral fin. In a few cases each year tails are broken.

This is wrong. Anyone who fishes for carp should have a net that's big enough to land them easily. A carp's weight should be equally dispersed when it's being carried from the water to the mat, and the netting itself should be soft and made from 'micromesh' type material.

If you're a beginner and are unsure of what net to buy, see what the tackle dealer recommends — but always go for a net that has the softest, smallest mesh in its base. That way you can't go too far wrong.

Try and get a net that has a diameter across its arms of around 40 inches minimum.

Tip Three
Breaking Down

With your carp safely landed in the net, take the arms of the net out of the spreader block. If you can, break the landing net handle down, too. I use a two-piece carbon landing net handle that comes apart easily. It makes handling carp of all sizes that little bit easier, just after netting.

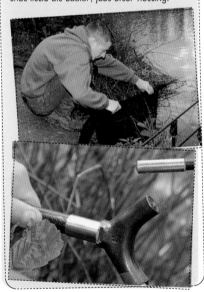

Tip Four
Soft-Actioned Rods

You might think that carp care starts on the bank. But you'd be wrong. In my view damage can occur when anglers use rods that are far too strong for the size of fish and type of waters they are fishing.

Soft rods absorb the lunges hooked carp make and are less likely to rip hooks from mouths, especially when fishing close in. Don't use 3.5lb test-curve rods when fishing close in or when stalking! On the small day ticket waters most of us fish, there really isn't any need for a rod that exceeds 2.5lb or 2.75lb test curve.

Tip Five
Wash And Go

I always wash my hands before handling a carp of any size. Our hands can get covered in all sorts of chemicals — from sources as bizarre as hair gel and petrol.

I remember seeing the famous old leather carp Heather from the Car Park Lake at Yateley on the bank once. She had two red marks on her belly, one under her head and the other by her anal fin — exactly where an angler's hands would have held her.

It's possible that our hands, if they're dry and if they have some dodgy chemicals on them, could injure carp. Therefore, I always wash my hands before fishing, using silt and weed from the lake. This also prevents any nasty smells getting on my bait. This can only help my angling!

Tip Six
Arrival

When you arrive in your chosen swim, don't wait until you have caught a fish before you start thinking about carp safety. Think about how you'll care for the fish you might catch before you even set your rods up.

On arriving in a swim, I like to visualise where I will unhook any fish I catch. I will firstly put my unhooking mat in a flat area, away from stones and hard ground if possible. Then I'll set up my landing net and position it in the spot where I think I can land a fish easily and safely. Only when all this is sorted will I set my rods up and cast them out.

Tip Seven
Secure Your Fish

Rather than sack fish up for 20 minutes to prepare for a photo, I think it's better to secure it in deep marginal water in your landing net. How do you do this?

Again, it comes down to preparation in advance. Before I land a carp, I attach a rod butt rest to the end of a storm stick and put it in the margins. The landing net rests on this while I'm waiting for a bite. After I have netted my carp, I will leave the fish in the net, in the water, and will place the net on the butt rest. To ensure the fish can't swim off with the net, I'll pin the back of the landing net handle down with a heavy bucket or a tent peg. I can also double check that my unhooking mat is wet and that I am fully ready to deal with the fish when it's on the bank.

I never sack fish in the UK any more. There isn't any need. I would advise all Let's Go Carp Fishing readers NEVER to use sacks! They're just too dangerous if used incorrectly, especially in the summer.

Tip Eight
Is Everything Prepared?

With the fish secured in the net for a couple of minutes, do some more checks. Make sure your mat is wet with cold lake water. Never put carp on a dry mat, especially if it's hot from the sun. That can cause real damage.

If you're going to weigh your carp, wet your sling. Take the chance now to zero your scales, too.

Tip Nine
Safety Tools

I always place several safety tools by the side of the mat in case I need them.

Firstly, forceps. I have a pair of curved and a pair of straight forceps. These are vital for getting hooks out that are either firmly lodged in the mouth, or hooks that might be a way back inside the mouth. I always carry a pair of wire cutters, too.

Occasionally, to get a hook out safely, you will need to cut it in half. You don't need these cutters very often but when you do they can really help you get a hook out of a carp without inflicting any damage at all.

Finally, I always take some antiseptic with me to treat any wounds on the fish I catch. All this is placed by the side of the mat at the start of the session.

Tip Ten
Carrying Your Fish

When it comes to lifting your fish out of the water, ensure that the pectoral fins are lying flush with the fish's body along the base of the net. If either of these fins are pointing in the wrong direction when you lift the carp from the water, they could snap. A carp without a pair of working pectoral fins is a carp that will find it hard to swim and feed.

Also, make sure that the weight of the carp is adequately and evenly supported in the bottom of the net. Its weight should not be resting on the tail, or on the head. I have occasionally seen carp with damaged tails caused when anglers have lifted them out of the water incorrectly. Tail lobes can split or snap in this situation. Most damage to carp occurs when carrying the fish from the lake to the mat, so make sure you know how to do it properly!

Tip Eleven
Sling Yer Bling

Before handling any fish for photos, take off any watches or rings on your wrist/fingers. These can get caught on various parts of the fish and remove scales or split fins. If you can't remove a ring from your finger, for whatever reason, then cover it with insulation tape. There's no way it can cause any damage this way. So ditch the bling!

Tip Twelve
Unhooking And Antiseptic

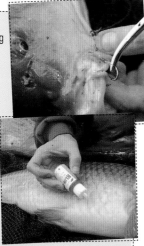

Be careful when unhooking a fish! If you can't gently ease the hook out with your fingers, use a pair of forceps and very carefully extract the hook. Try and ease it out of the hole in the same way it entered. In this way you will minimise any chance of damage being caused to the fish's mouth.

When the carp has been successfully unhooked, examine it carefully for any missing scales or split fins. Get out your antiseptic and apply a little using a cotton bud to any areas you think might need it. Don't overdo it, though. You don't need much antiseptic, a small dab is more than adequate. Never touch the fish's eyes with the stuff and avoid touching the barbules with it as well – these are very sensitive areas for a fish!

I think all carp anglers should carry either Klin-Ik or Fish Doctor as a matter of course.

Tip Thirteen
Holding Your Fish

If you hold your fish properly, there shouldn't be any problem getting a good catch pic without your fingers being spread across the fish's flank!

Depending on what you find more comfortable, hold your carp like this: firstly, place your left hand under the back of the carp's head – right underneath its gills. If you need to stop the fish sliding around, gently place the pectoral fin between your fingers.

Secondly, place your right hand by the anal fin. You can see in the picture that the fin is gently sandwiched between my fingers.

Finally, a good tip is to watch the gills. An advance sign that the carp is going to flip is when the gills start to flare and move more quickly. This usually precedes the fish having a bit of a panic attack, so if you feel the fish tense up and see the gills move faster, put it down on the mat. Let it calm down. Covering its eyes with a damp cloth can help. Pour some cool lake water over it to keep it damp before picking it up again.

When holding your fish for a photo, keep it quite low to the ground directly above the mat. Never stand up with a carp. Accidents can happen; a carp can be dropped by the most experienced angler when it suddenly flips. If your carp is low to the ground and above a well-padded mat when you drop it, it will be fine. If it's some way above the ground, you could kill it if you drop it. So be careful!

Tip Fourteen
Trophy Shot

I weigh my fish after I've done the photo. That way I can use the weigh sling to return the fish. The less you put a carp in and out of a weigh sling or sack the better, as this can remove some of the fish's protective slime.

Digital photography has helped with carp care. These days, you can get a decent camera with a self-take facility for a couple of hundred quid. The ability to see the picture you've just taken is excellent, as you can frame your picture perfectly before the carp is even on the mat. All I do is put my camera on a bucket and frame the shot up above the unhooking mat. Then I'll pose with nothing in my hands, taking a picture or two with my remote-control button. Before I put the carp on the mat I'll check the dummy-run picture to ensure I've got it right.

With practice, you can take brilliant self-take trophy shots. Gone is the need for carp sacks!

Self-Take Digital Trophy Shot

1

First, put a camera on a bucket, or something similar, and frame the shot up.

2

Now move above the mat and take a picture using a remote control.

Check the picture is well framed. Now get the carp and pose in the same spot.

Tip Fifteen
Weighing Your Fish

Weighing Your Fish

Before you lift the carp from the water your weigh sling should be wet, cool and right next to your mat. So should all the unhooking tools and antiseptics you might need, along with your scales.

Make sure the mat is cool and wet, then carefully carry the fish over to it. Lay the fish on the mat and remove the net, placing the fish in the weigh sling if you want to weigh it.

Before lifting the fish in the sling, check again that its fins are flush to its body. Then, with the scales attached to the cords on the sling, slowly lift the fish off the ground, letting the scales take the weight.

In case anything goes wrong, make sure you don't lift the carp too high off the ground. A couple of inches off the mat is all you need to get a reading on the scales. Then, if something goes wrong (like the cord on the sling snapping, for instance) the carp won't have far to fall onto the mat and will not be harmed.

Always weigh your fish directly over a thick, padded mat!

1 Before lifting the fish from the water ensure your mat's wet and the sling is close by.

2 Lift the fish from the water and transfer it from the net to the mat.

3 Put the fish in the sling and check that its fins are lying flush with its body.

4 Hook the sling onto your scales and lift it a few inches off the ground, over your mat.

Tip Sixteen
Returning Your Carp

When it comes to putting your carp back in the lake, never carry it over rough ground in your hands. It doesn't matter how small the fish is, don't do it!

I use my mat to return the fish. My Nix Angling mat has a Velcro-fastening flap covering its entire surface area. This flap holds the carp in position so it cannot get off the mat. I simply secure the fish inside the flap and carry it to the water's edge.

Finally, a good tip to revive a tired fish is to hold onto its tails and gently pull it backwards and forwards, stimulating water flow through its gills. This usually gets it to kick and swim away strongly. Always support the fish in the water until it's ready to swim off of its own accord.

Mastermind

Dave Lane, one of the country's best carp anglers, answers questions on all things carpy.

Q What effect does the heat have on a sacked fish, and when is it safe to sack one?

A In the heat of the day, the oxygen levels in the water will be at their lowest and this is the most dangerous time to sack a fish. A sacked fish needs a good transfer of water and oxygen through the mesh of the sack to keep it healthy and fit. On a calm, baking-hot day this is difficult to achieve.

There is rarely a reason to sack a fish in daytime. If it needs to be retained for a short period it is often better to peg out the landing net and leave the fish in it.

Have your photography and unhooking equipment set up in advance, to minimise the time a fish is out of the water.

Factors such as strength of wind, depth of water, clarity of water and oxygen levels should all be considered before sacking a carp. Allow the fish enough cord so it can lay on the bottom if it wants.

Margins that are turbulent, coloured or silted up can cause problems if the sack mesh becomes clogged with particles. Weed and lily pads should also be avoided as they can use up massive amounts of oxygen and the fish can also become entangled while sacked.

In general, sacking fish at night for short

Keep all of these to hand, if possible.

periods is acceptable in clear, well-oxygenated and sheltered water, away from snags, weed and shallow margins. However, if you are in any doubt, or the fish is stressed or suffering in any way, then just put it straight back.

Sacking A Carp For Short Periods

1 Ensure you have a large, good quality sack.

2 Zip the carp in the sack, being careful not to catch its fins.

3 If you can lock the zip shut, as you can on the JRC sack, do so.

4 Place the sack in a deep, sheltered margin.

5 Securely fasten the sack to a bankstick or storm pole.

6 Once you're ready to deal with the carp, lift it from the water.

7 Weigh and photograph your catch as quickly as possible.

8 Return the carp safely to the water using your mat.

Erm, what shall I use today?

The Bait Baron

With so many carp baits on the market, choosing the right one can prove difficult. To help you decide, bait expert Ian Russell tells you which baits he uses, when he uses them and why.

Many anglers will tell you that bait selection is down to personal preference and that you should use whatever bait you have confidence in. While confidence is an important factor in your bait choice and baiting approach, there are other factors to consider which can often dictate how successful your session is.

Rather than give you a set of 'rules' to follow, I'll explain what baits I use, when I use them and why. That way you can make your own mind up as to what's best because, let's face it, carp never follow the rules anyway.

Many anglers see particles only as a summer approach but I use them from the start of spring right through to the

first frost. They're a very cheap and easy way of mass baiting, especially if you buy them in bulk and prepare them yourself. And they'll keep the carp occupied for hours. My favourite particle mix, which I use 90 per cent of the time, is a simple aniseed, pigeon-conditioning feed to which I add sweetcorn, a few tiger nuts and peanuts

Particle Bags

1

Using a towel, dry a small handful of your chosen particles.

2

Place the dried particles into a length of PVA stocking.

3

Tie the bag off tightly. Ian always doubles over his PVA.

4

Attach the bag to your hook and you're ready to go.

– where allowed, of course. This mix contains so many different bits and pieces of various sizes, shapes and weights that the carp have difficulty singling out the hook bait and invariably end up eating it.

If the venue I'm fishing holds a big head of carp and if I'm expecting multiple catches, then I have no hesitation in putting lots of particles into my swim. If there are only a few carp in the water and I'm fishing for one bite at a time, then I'd opt for a much more conservative baiting approach. Remember, small fish will demolish a lot of what you put in. The attentions of nuisance fish are the major downside to using particles and, if there is a large head of bream or tench in the water, then I would be reluctant to use them. If I'm only after one take, then I try to keep the bait as tight as possible rather than scattering it around. The idea is to concentrate the carp into as small an area as possible to increase your chances of a pick-up.

On venues that are rarely fished and where the carp will have seen very few boilies, particles would be my number-one choice. For some reason particles seem to be more readily accepted, but I would add a few boilies into the mix to try and get the carp used to them. When fishing over a bed of particles, my favourite hook baits are tiger nuts and maize. They're very reliable, the carp love them and they withstand the attentions of nuisance fish. The only problem with using particles on the hair is that they're very light and can cause the hair or hooklength to tangle on the cast. One way around this problem is to attach a small PVA bag of particles to the hook. Yes, you did read that right; you can use particles inside PVA bags, providing that you dry them off first.

When carp are feeding over a bed of particles they move very slowly, often remaining upended on one spot for a while. In this situation a long hooklength will work against you. A short hooklength of four or five inches will result in many more carp on the bank in this instance.

Although particles are an excellent bait, boilies are by far my favourites to use. They're extremely convenient, as they require no preparation, and can be used straight from the packet. The main advantage of using a quality boilie is that it's a great food source. The carp can tell the difference between a good and a poor-quality bait and, given the choice, will opt for the good-quality bait every time. This is why a quality frozen bait is ideal for a baiting campaign. If I ever put a large amount of boilies into a

Alter the shape of your baits.

This one fell for a boilie – carp can't get enough of them.

Particles, cheap and very effective.

water then I would use frozen baits every time. While there are some high-quality, shelf-life baits available, I don't believe that they're as good as frozen baits, which is why I rarely use them. Boilies are also one of the most selective baits out there as far as carp are concerned. In fact, I've caught hundreds of carp by laying down a bed of particles, to attract as many fish as possible, and then putting a bed of boilies over the top. The commotion caused by the small fish attacking the particles should attract the carp to the area, where there's a bed of boilies waiting for them.

You only have to look in the freezer at your local tackle shop to see how many different freezer baits are available. Therefore, choosing a bait to

> CARP LEARN BY ASSOCIATION AND CAN BECOME WARY OF ROUND BAITS.

suit you can be a bit of a hit-and-miss affair. The easiest way to choose a bait is to keep your eyes on the catch reports in angling publications and to ask around on the water that you're fishing to see what other anglers are catching on. In this way not only will you know that the bait you're using catches fish but you will also benefit from other anglers baiting up. Freezer baits might cost a little more than some others on offer but bait is

one area where you shouldn't tighten the purse strings.

Because carp learn by association they can become wary of round baits. Try and make your baits a little different, whether that's changing the shape or even the size. You'll be amazed at the difference it makes.

At Heathrow Bait Services I get a lot of people phoning up asking me questions about bait. One of the most popular questions is about colour and whether it makes a difference to a bait's effectiveness. In coloured water I don't think colour makes a lot of difference due to the low visibility. However, in clear water I prefer to use dull or lightly coloured baits. I'm sure that a big bed of bright baits in clear water will glow like a warning beacon and probably spook the fish. Having said that, I would have no hesitation using a single, bright pop-up over a bed of dull freebies purely for curiosity value, as carp are nosey buggers!

Using a lot of bait isn't always the best option and single hook baits are excellent for opportunist fishing. A single bait cast at a showing fish will often get you a quick bite. I always prefer to use hi-viz pop-ups for single-bait fishing as I'm looking for instant attraction.

When casting at showing fish, you rarely know what you're fishing over. Here, I prefer to use pop-ups as they sit on top of any bottom debris, providing you're not casting into thick weed or very deep silt. Single hook baits also score well when there are already fish in the area, such as when fishing

Glugged pellets won't absorb smells from the lake bed.

When using PVA stringers, always leave a gap between the baits...

... or the water can't attack the PVA and it won't dissolve.

Minimal Baiting Approaches

1

2

3

Approach One
Small PVA bags of pellets score well when heavy baiting isn't working.

Approach Two
PVA bags of oil-based glugs provide loads of attraction but little food.

Approach Three
Small PVA stocking bags of pellets are a very popular choice all year round.

against snags. There's little point in chucking mountains of bait into an area where there's already plenty of fish. Nine times out of 10 this will work against you.

Along with boilies, my other favourite bait is pellets. I use them on every venue I fish and have no hesitation in putting absolutely loads of them out. The carp love them and once they get their heads down they keep feeding until there's nothing left. The only time I would keep the amount of pellets to a minimum is when there's a big head of tench and bream. I don't use dry pellets straight from the packet; I like to make my pellets different to everybody else's. Dry pellets act like a sponge once they're in the water and if you're fishing over silt or a smelly lake bed then the pellets will become impregnated with the smell as they take on water. To avoid this I soak my pellets in oil. You can use any oil or glug, such as salmon oil, CSL or HBS Hydro Stim. All you need to do is put 5kg of pellets into a bucket along with 500ml of your chosen liquid and let the pellets absorb it, giving the bucket a shake now and then to ensure the liquid is evenly distributed. Once the pellets have soaked up all the liquid, I add a few handfuls of crushed hemp, which sticks to the pellets and just gives them a little extra attraction.

As well as being a great boost for your pellets, glugs are excellent for increasing the attraction of your hook bait. You can leave your hook baits in a pot of glug for weeks, or just give your hook bait a quick dip before you cast

Carp are curious creatures and will investigate a bright pop-up.

out to boost its attraction. A PVA bag of glug is another way to boost the attraction of your hook bait but make sure that the glug is oil based, as water-based glugs will melt PVA. This is a great tactic in the winter when you want loads of attraction in your swim but very little food.

A common problem that hundreds of anglers face at the start of every session is how much bait to put in.

Unfortunately, there are no hard-and-fast rules to follow; it's just a case of reading the water and establishing what the carp want on the day. I know that's probably not the information you wanted, but that's the way it is. This judgement is down to watercraft, which can only come through

This one fell to a big bed of boilies.

experience and spending time at the water. However, there are a few rough guidelines that you can follow. For example, if it's red hot and flat calm then the chances are the carp aren't going to feed hard. If this is the case, then little bags, PVA stringers or a few pouchfuls of feed will suffice.

On the other hand, if it's overcast and stormy and the carp are crashing out all over the lake then you can get away with putting a fair bit of bait in.

Through the summer and autumn I get through mountains of bait, especially when the weather's right. It's always worth carrying a couple of extra buckets of bait in the back of your car just in case. If the carp really start having it, then you don't want to run out. Having a couple of extra buckets available may just get you a few more carp. If you don't use it, obviously you can always take it home and use it on your next session. It's always best to have too much bait than not enough.

A stunning mid-double taken on a stringer.

Mastermind

Dave Lane, one of the country's best carp anglers, answers questions on all things carpy.

Choose a bait with a good track record.

Q Although you're sponsored by Mainline baits, is there a frozen boilie range that you could recommend and what do you look for in a quality boilie?

A Yes you are quite right, I am sponsored by Mainline and have been exclusively using its baits for more years than I care to mention, so I can only realistically recommend baits from its range. However, in saying that, I can't really recommend them highly enough, as they have done me no end of good over the years and I have total confidence in all of them. When choosing a freezer bait that you intend using over a period of time, I would always pick a reputable company that has a track record of producing quality baits. 'Food source' baits, as they are often termed, should supply the fish with a range of dietary requirements and also include triggers to promote a feeding response. There is a lot more to bait formulation than just a pile of fishmeals and a squirt of the newest flavour!

With the Mainline baits, such as the Fusion that I currently use, water acts as the catalyst that will create a reaction within the bait itself, quickly breaking down the nutrients and releasing a signal for the carp to home in on. A good freezer bait should not hang around on the bottom of the lake for weeks if not eaten, and I prefer it if they either float up after a few days or break down to a state where small fish and invertebrates can polish them off. I also like to have a whole range of baits made from the same ingredients as the boilies – pellets of different sizes and breakdown rates, bait dips and, of course, pop-ups, which all match my chosen bait.

Basically, if you ascertain which baits are catching regularly and which companies have a good, reliable name and stick to those, you won't go far wrong. It's tempting to search out a more obscure bait in the hope that it may just be the wonderbait you've been looking for but, take it from me, the more of a quality bait that fish see and eat, the better it becomes. By using an established recipe, you're benefiting from the baiting up of others and helping to give the carp even more confidence in eating that particular bait.

Q Why do single hook baits work? There's no way a 14mm, bright-yellow ball, sat just above the lake bed and smelling of pineapple, can resemble natural food. Also, when's the best time to use single hook baits?

A Using single, bright, smelly yellow hook baits, or any colour really, can actually be a very effective method of catching fish that are happily feeding on natural baits.

I think what happens is that they tend to suck in practically everything that looks interesting around the area where they are feeding, rejecting those items that they don't want. If your hook bait is among those items, and your rig is working effectively, then the rest will be history.

Single pop-ups have caught me a string of fish over the years and they have many different applications.

Fishing on top of gravel bars in summer when the fish are using them as a patrol route is a classic example. Casting at rolling fish when you don't want the disturbance of a marker float and spod is another.

You don't necessarily have to use pop-ups either. A lot of anglers seem to equate single-bait fishing with buoyant baits, but I have had a lot of success with bottom baits too.

Rigs for single-bait fishing need not be overly complicated, because the fish have no real point of reference when they are not feeding on similar food items, as they do with a bed of boilies.

A standard pop-up rig with counterbalance weight is ideal, as shown in the photograph. As for single, bottom baits, I tend to stick to either a coated hook link with no breaks or a straightforward nylon hook link.

These simple rigs can be very effective because they sit nicely over whatever type of bottom they may land on.

In fact, many good fish I have caught recently have fallen to single baits, both pop-ups and 12mm bottom baits.

Casting single hook baits at rolling fish has caught me plenty, including some big ones.

High-attract, single hook baits can be very effective.

Keep it simple.

Cheap As *Chips*

There are ways of making what you spend on carp baits go a very long way, as legendary tightwad Neil Smith shows Marc Coulson.

Now, I am not saying that Neil Smith is tight, but he has his trousers tailored with especially long pockets. If he could shorten his arms too, I am sure he would! The propensity of the Wigan wonder to get away with spending as little as possible is legendary and he was the natural choice for a feature about carp angling on a budget.

I'd arranged to meet Neil at Lymm Angling Club's Belmont Pool in my home county of Cheshire. The time of our rendezvous is set at 4pm and, as I look at my watch, I despair as he his already half an hour late.

NEIL SAYS THAT ALL THE STUFF HE HAS BOUGHT WILL LAST FOR A VERY LONG TIME.

Fortunately, Lymm bailiff Paul Rylance, who is accompanying us on the trip, is already at the water and so I make my way down to find him set up in the area called 'the woods'. As I approach, one of Paul's alarms screams out and he is soon playing a Belmont carp.

As Paul lands the carp, he tells me that it

ANGLER FILE

Name: Neil Smith
Age: 39
Hometown: Wigan
UK PB: 34lb 4oz

is his fourth capture in a little over a couple of hours – the water is on fire and I cannot wait to get a bait cast out. I take a quick snap of the fish and go back to the car park to get my gear.

I'm soon set up in the middle of the woods and ring Neil to find out where he is. He's just pulling into the car park and asks me to go and give him a hand with all the sacks of bait he has brought with him.

I wonder what the hell he is on about, but oblige.

"Just how long are you lads planning on staying?" asks another angler, who is just loading his car up before leaving.

I look round to see Neil buried under a

mountain of huge sacks that appear to be full of animal food!

"There you go, there's nearly 100kg dry weight of bait here for less than 40 quid. That 100kg of dry weight can easily double in size once wet and prepared," Neil proclaims.

Sure enough, he hands me the receipts for the sacks (yep, I'm paying him for the bait he's bought for the feature) and I notice that the amount is a paltry £38.76.

Neil isn't lying about the amount of bait, and takes me through what he's got. There are big sacks of barley, groats, pigeon feed, goat feed, Vitalin and dog biscuits.

Barley and groats are long-time favourites of many carp anglers and Vitalin

All this oil for just a few quid, and it'll last for ages.

You can get all this for less than £60 if you shop in the right places.

Neils hopes for a change of fortune.

Mixed Corn

COUNTRYSIDE

Super Solvitax, which is basically pure cod liver oil that is used to supplement the diet of horses.

Neil tells me: "Oils seem to be all the rage in carp fishing at the moment and this stuff is an excellent base to many bag mixes, groundbaits and spod mixes. If you were to buy many of the fish oils from tackle shops they would set you back considerably more than this stuff.

"I have paid £13 for this – my most expensive purchase – and there is enough here to last most anglers up to six months."

That is an important point to mention here – this quantity of bait is not just for today's feature and Neil is right when he says that all the stuff he has bought will last for a very long time.

"I am not suggesting for one minute that all these should replace the baits that we all use. However, they can be used very effectively to bulk out the more expensive stuff, such as boilies, pellets and tiger nuts," Neil continues.

I ask Neil to pose for a picture with all the baits so that readers can see exactly what a large amount of bait a small amount of money can buy.

As we put the sacks back in his car – Neil has already sorted some out into buckets for today's session – I ask him where he bought all the gear from.

"I have an animal-feed retailer near to me which sells bulk foods to farmers and horse owners, but you can get most of these from large pet food shops.

"You may have to find a bigger place for the Super Solvitax but the rest can almost certainly be found in your local 'Pets Are Us'."

So, in all, there is enough bait here to last some anglers a whole year – and all for less than £60.

I once came here with Neil and did a feature for Advanced Carp Fishing, when we both worked on the best-selling specimen carp title. The carp that day responded to a bit of bait and Neil is hoping that the same is true today.

Neil has an island in front of him and notes a small hole in the overhanging bushes. "That has to be a hotspot, because carp love such cover, especially over island margins," he explains.

Neil doesn't mind being woken in the night for one of these.

dry dog food is also a real winner. The goat feed is very similar to Vitalin. If you look at the ingredients closely you will find all the things that carp anglers use regularly, such as hemp, maize, dari seeds and lots more. Pigeon feed has also been used by lots of thrifty carp anglers, instead of some of the more expensive mixed particles that you can buy.

As well as the dry bait, Neil has also purchased a 3l bottle of molasses – a sweet syrup that has a real pedigree as a carp attractor. This molasses cost less than a fiver, which is exceptional when you consider that you can pay that for 500ml of molasses from many tackle shops!

Together with the molasses, Neil has also got a similar-sized drum of something called

He sets about mixing some of his budget baits ready to spod into the swim. There are all sorts of bits going into the mix and Neil doesn't need to be too tight, seeing as the bait has cost him next to nothing.

Neil points out one very important aspect of using these particle baits, as he explains: "It is vital that you don't just use these baits straight from the bag – they should always be presoaked first. The softer particles like the groats should be soaked at least overnight before you go fishing. The harder barley and wheat should be soaked for a little longer, maybe another 12 hours or so.

"I take the Vitalin with me dry but boil up some lake water to mix it. This speeds up the soaking process and makes the whole mix much easier to combine.

"I also like to add the molasses at the early stages of mixing, as well as any other liquid attractors."

Neil mixes up a bucketful of his various baits and adds the molasses and some natural attractor from Star Baits. He also put in some Dynamite hemp and tiger nuts as well as some boilies.

As Neil sets about spodding his mix into the swim, I notice that Paul is into yet another Belmont carp, his seventh in fact.

> ## IT HAS LONG BAFFLED ME HOW A CARP CAN TRANSFER A HOOK INTO A SNAG.

The evening is drawing to a close and we set about preparing for the night ahead. Neil's spot that he has spodded the bait out to is fizzing with bubbles and he receives a number of line bites.

After an hour or so the bubbles stop and the line bites also dry up. Neil decides to spod some more gear out to the spot and within minutes the area starts to fizz once more.

"I am sure that the carp in here want

A proper 'Cheshire' mirror at 20lb 10oz.

A change of swim proved productive.

Neil treats a slight wound with some Klin-Ik antiseptic.

some food and I reckon they've cleaned me out. I might be facing a night of spodding and respodding in order to keep fish in the area," Neil states.

As darkness approaches, his right-hand rod roars off. Because his baited rigs are so close to the far marginal snags, Neil is sitting close to his rods and is on it in a flash.

The fish feels heavy and manages to get its head into some overhanging foliage. Neil is powerless to stop the fish and eventually the angry carp sheds the rig, depositing it in a snag.

I comment that it has long baffled me how a carp, which does not have hands, can transfer a hook from its mouth into a snag so often. A disappointed Neil decides not to comment and I leave him to lick his wounds.

Big Paul gets some curry on the go and Neil recasts his rig. Just as the curry is ready and I am licking my lips in anticipation, my margin rod rattles off. All three of us jump up, not immediately sure whose alarm it is that's screaming out.

I am gutted as, after a good 10-minute fight, the fish comes off. I am horrified when I swing my rig back in to find that my 15lb Sink Link has snapped clean in two, halfway down my hook link.

The night is an eventful one, as Neil lands a nice mirror and loses another two. I manage to winkle out a mid-double and, while unhooking and returning it, I notice that Paul has wound all three rods in. I guess he wants some sleep after his hectic hauling.

While Neil has got off the mark, as well as losing a couple, we both discuss him moving into Paul's swim once the big lad packs up. He will be leaving in the morning due to the 24-hour rule and we both agree that a move is on the cards.

In true Smithy fashion, he has not brought any storm caps for his brolly and nicks the front two off mine. If I had a pound for every time this man has 'borrowed' gear from me I'd be a rich man.

You don't need a lot of bait to catch a carp or two.

Neil's Budget Spod Mix

Neil adds liquid molasses to a bucket of Vitalin dog food. Molasses is a real carp puller.

He then boils some lake water and adds a small amount to the bucket.

Use more expensive ingredients sparingly. Here Neil adds half a jar of Dynamite Frenzied Hemp.

A jar of tiger nuts can also be made to go a long way by adding just a few at a time.

Neil rates barley as an excellent and cheap particle. You can buy this from animal-feed stores.

Chicken feed contains many particles that are used in carp fishing.

The whole lot is mixed thoroughly so that the water starts to bind it.

Last of all add whatever liquid attractors you like. This is a potent booster that Neil rates.

Typically, given this fact, the heavens open that night and I have to fumble around to pull my brolly down over me as I cannot attach any poles – due to my lack of caps! Neil is okay, though, and has poles up and sleeps as snug as a bug in a rug.

Unusually, we are both glad that we receive no further action through the rainy night and wake the next morning with our rigs still out on their respective spots.

Paul is slowly packing away his kit but has slung one rod out to his island spot. It isn't long before it rips off and Paul lands his 16th carp of the session.

He isn't recasting, so I beckon Neil into Paul's swim. He doesn't need asking twice, as it is blatantly obvious that most of the lake's carp are round that side of the island. This is an important factor when day ticket fishing – if someone is leaving a productive swim, don't be afraid to move in behind them.

Neil slings a couple of spodfuls of bait to the productive area and soon has carp fizzing over the gear.

"This is more like it. Paul has had loads of carp from here to 19lb and I really fancy our chances of adding a couple to our tally," Neil tells me.

Sure enough, one of Neil's rods rips off and this time he is not going to let it get away. He soon brings it buder control and

has the fish wallowing up and down the margins beneath his feet.

"This sort of behaviour under rod tips is often the sign of a good fish," Neil whispers, not wanting to tempt fate too much.

More bait? Er no, this is Neil's breakfast.

As the carp tires and is teased over the net cord, it is obvious that Neil is right. This thought is confirmed as Smithy heaves the fish and landing net out of the water and onto his waiting mat.

Paul is keen to weigh the fish quickly and we are all thrilled as the needle passes 20lb, finally settling on 20lb 10oz. It's a stunner too – a typical Cheshire carp and a rare one too, at more than 20lb.

We make the carp famous with a few snaps and Neil treats an old wound on one of its flanks with some Klin-Ik. The magnificent fish is soon slipped back and, in true carp-angler fashion, we thank it for obliging us.

Neil has not only proved that his budget-bait approach catches carp but also that it catches big carp and, for the second feature in a row, we've a had a right result with a well-earned twenty.

"There's a bit of a pattern emerging here, Neil," I point out with a wry smile.

"Yes marra, these last two captures have, in a strange kind of way, been very similar! I cannot wait 'til next time we're out," comes the reply.

Be a Master Caster

ANGLER FILE

Name: Steve Spurgeon
Age: 39
UK PB: 41lb 6oz
Occupation: Company Director, Korda

ANGLER FILE

Name: Chris Rose
Age: 39
UK PB: 41lb 2oz
Occupation: Company Director, Korda

Chris Rose and Steve Spurgeon show Marc Coulson how you can improve your casting technique.

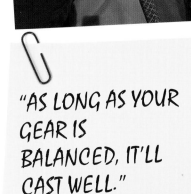

Mono or braid – it's your choice.

Why is everybody obsessed with being able to cast as far as possible? And why do so many carp anglers insist on chucking rigs out as far as they possibly can every time they go fishing? Not sure of the answer? No, it's a mystery to me as well!

I have lost count of how many times I've wandered the banks and seen anglers fishing at 100 yards and more when there are obviously lots of carp within a gentle lob of where they stand.

The other classic is to see anglers absolutely busting a gut to hit the horizon with no consideration of how accurate or, rather, inaccurate their casts are.

The casting features I see in the fishing magazines always seem to revolve around getting a 5oz or 6oz lead out further than I go on my holidays! However, they rarely highlight the very basic casting techniques that we all require.

With this in mind, I find myself at Drayton Reservoir along with the Korda boys, Chris Rose and Steve Spurgeon.

Both anglers are known for their casting prowess and each can sling a lead to infinity and beyond. However, they share my belief that many anglers get the basics of casting wrong and that not enough attention is paid to casting technique.

"It's not all about casting as far as you can. It's far more important to be as accurate as possible," Chris tells me, as I nod my head in agreement.

"What's the point in being able to cast

"AS LONG AS YOUR GEAR IS BALANCED, IT'LL CAST WELL."

150 yards if every cast lands 20 yards to the left or right of your marker? I know a few anglers who can cast a long way, but ask them to flick it 40 yards and tight to a marker float and they need three or four attempts," Steve adds.

We are here to look at the basic elements of casting with a carp rod – get these right and you can then go on and practise getting your lead to fly further and further.

The obvious place to start is with the tackle the boys are using. Chris has his 13ft 3.5lb test curve Greys Platinum rods and big Shimano Power Aero reels.

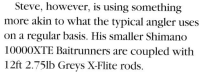

Aim the rod butt at your target for accurate casting.

Steve, however, is using something more akin to what the typical angler uses on a regular basis. His smaller Shimano 10000XTE Baitrunners are coupled with 12ft 2.75lb Greys X-Flite rods.

"As long as your gear is balanced, it'll cast well," Chris explains. "Yeah mate, although big-pit reels and big rods will cast further, you can still cast pretty well with a lighter set-up," chips in Steve.

It's true, and when you consider that most of us fish on smaller venues that do not require casts of more than 120 yards, the lighter set-up will suffice.

"If you think about it, this set-up was considered pretty strong gear only a few years ago. There's been a movement towards big reels and strong rods when, often, they are just not necessary," Steve adds.

I notice that Chris is using braided main line, so I ask him why. "I definitely get more yards with braid, although I only use it on venues where it is allowed, obviously. It's important to use the right braid, though. A heavy, sinking braid will not cast as well as a light, floating braid,"

Use a protective finger stall with braid.

Chris holds his rod and reel like this...

... whereas Steve's grip is slightly different.

he explains, adding: "Oh, always use a fingerstall with braid, otherwise you could seriously damage your fingers."

When we've finished looking at the gear the lads use, I ask them to each give me a couple of tips and also highlight what they believe are the key elements to casting. In a nutshell, I want to know what the most common faults are that they see with people's casting.

"I'll tell you one thing that loads of anglers get wrong, and that's the way they apply the pressure with each arm," says Steve.

"It's important that as well as pushing forwards with the right arm (in the case of a right-handed caster), they should also pull down with the left. This is what creates a lot of the power."

Perfect!

Feather the line as the rig hits the water.

Chris has his own 'favourite' fault, one that he often sees anglers getting wrong. "I would say that the weight distribution is a very important one, mate.

"I see so many anglers simply using their arms and hands to cast the rod, whereas the best casters use their legs as well. You should start with your weight pretty much on your back foot. As you bring the rod over your head, the weight should transfer forwards until, as you let go of the line and surge the rod forwards, most of the weight moves through onto the front foot. Any golfers out there will understand that one," Chris explains.

As well as the distance that these guys achieve, I notice just how accurate their casting is. Steve takes me through how this can be improved before the rod has even been cast. He explains: "A great tip for keeping the cast nice and straight is to point the butt at the target when holding the rod over your head. In this way, as you bring the rod forwards on the cast the lead will fly straight towards your chosen spot.

"Try not to make the cast until the lead has stopped waving around behind you. Wait for it to settle fairly still and this will also improve your accuracy."

There's more too, as Steve then talks about how much line should hang from the rod tip when getting ready to cast. This is called 'the drop' and is very important.

"If your drop is too short, you will not get the 'zip' into the cast and it will fly extremely low. This, more often than not,

Use Your Arms For Better Casting

1

2

3

With the rod behind you, ready to go, steady your arms before casting.

Move the rod back slightly before bringing it forward, creating a slingshot effect.

As well as pushing with your top arm, be sure to pull down with your bottom arm.

Transfer Your Weight For Distance

1

2

3

As the rod moves back, transfer your weight onto the back foot...

...before thrusting your weight forward as the rod comes over your head...

...and then push the rod forwards before the line starts to peel off the reel.

Find the right range and the action can be frantic.

1 Make a cast to your marker float and then trap the line in the clip.

2 Trap the line with a piece of electrical insulating tape, like this.

3 Fold the tape over the line and stick it firmly together.

4 Trim the tape with scissors, leaving a marker on your line. Job done

Steve and Chris both enjoy distance fishing for carp.

SOMETIMES, CASTING THAT LITTLE BIT FURTHER WILL GET YOU AN EXTRA BITE.

results in casts falling short. Too long a drop and your lead will be propelled skywards rather than forwards. Chris and I favour having the lead and rig hanging level with the spigot – the join between the two rod sections – which will mean a drop of about six feet.

"This will create a much better trajectory and give more consistent results. As an extension to this, I would say that you should always aim above your chosen target or far-bank marker. If you are aiming towards a tree, for instance, focusing on it will often lead to short casts. By looking, and aiming, at a point above the tree you will generally get a better trajectory and hit the distance more readily."

"How do you both make sure that you hit the right spot every time. Do you clip up?" I ask.

Chris takes over and shows me how you can ensure your casts hit the same spot on every occasion.

"This is the simplest way of doing it, I suppose," he tells me. "I'll cast to the spot and, once I am happy that it's right, I place the line in the clip on the spool of the reel to hold it in place. Then I stick a small piece of electrical insulation tape onto the line just above the reel. I trim this right down so that it can fly through

the rod rings easily.

"Next, the line comes out of the clip so that I can fish safely. If I have to recast without having caught a fish, I simply pop the line back into the clip. If I have caught one and I need to recast, it is slightly different. I cast out away from the area I am fishing and, as soon as I feel the tape flicking through the rings, I feather the line and stop it in its tracks. I then retrieve enough line so that the tape is back in position, just above the reel. The line goes back into the clip and I wind in, ready to recast.

"I then cast at my target and hold the rod

up nice and high. As the line hits the clip and stops the rig, I cushion the impact by bringing the rod forward. It might all sound a bit long-winded, but it's pretty simple and effective really," he concludes.

So that you can all see how easy it can be, we take some pictures to show how Chris creates the tape marker on the line.

As we do, each angler has a flurry of action and both are into Drayton carp. After the obligatory grip-and-grin shots, we decide that we've pretty much exhausted the casting feature and retire to the nearby pub. Now, that's what I call top angling!

Tip One
Choose The Right Lead

The right sort of lead is essential, and the shape and type are vital for getting the best from every cast. Swivel leads are best, but if you must use an inline version, use one that has its weight nearest the nose, as shown on the right.

Tip Two
Get Riggy

Helicopter rigs will cast furthest, as the lead flies out before the rig and hook bait. If you are not sure how tie helicopter rigs, use a lead-clip system instead. Be sure to use some form of anti-tangle leader.

Tip Three
Match Up

Using the biggest lead doesn't necessarily mean longer casts. Roughly match your lead to the test curve of your rod. For example, a 3oz lead with a 2.75lb rod is ideal.

Tip Four
Get The Right Leader

When it comes to choosing your anti-tangle leader, shorter ones will fly further than long ones. Don't use leadcore, as it is too heavy and the extra weight will hinder your casting potential. The pre-tied Korda ones are ideal.

Tip Five
Not Too Long, Not Too Short

The length of the drop between your rod tip and your rig is an important factor in your ability to make good, consistent casts. Too short and your casts will fly low, too long and they go too high. Try a drop of around six feet.

Tip Six
Stick It To 'Em

Single hook baits will cast further than PVA bags or sticks. If you insist on using bags or sticks, use smaller ones – they fly further. Use just three-bait PVA stringers too.

Tip Seven
Shocker!

If you really want to fish at long range, you will need to use some form of shockleader, to ensure that the stress does not cause your main line to snap. Most leader materials will include instructions on how to tie them.

Tip Eight
Don't Fill Up

If and when you start to use spods, don't overfill them. By having too much bait in the spod, the aerodynamics are reduced. Have a gap at the back, which means the weight is more towards the nose. This will fly much further and straighter than a spod which is packed too full. Give it a try.

GET SERIOUS – GET

£3,000 WORTH OF PRIZES MUST BE WON INSIDE

The magazine for the ultra-dedicated angler obsessed by carp and carp fishing. The biggest names, the biggest fish and the biggest stories.

MARCH 2006 £3.

A DHP PUBLICAT

Advanced CARP Fishing

WATER WORLD
Pete Castle dips below the surface to help you catch

EXCLUSIVE
THE FAB FOUR
LEE JACKSON
DAVE GAWTHORN
LEON BARTROPP
JIM SHELLEY

TWO FORTIES IN 40 MINUTES
...ve Moore's exclusive story

UNSPONSORED RIG BLITZ
What's hot and what's not

ON SALE
THE SECOND FRIDAY OF EACH MONTH

OME SERIOUS HELP!

ON SALE
THE LAST FRIDAY OF EACH MONTH

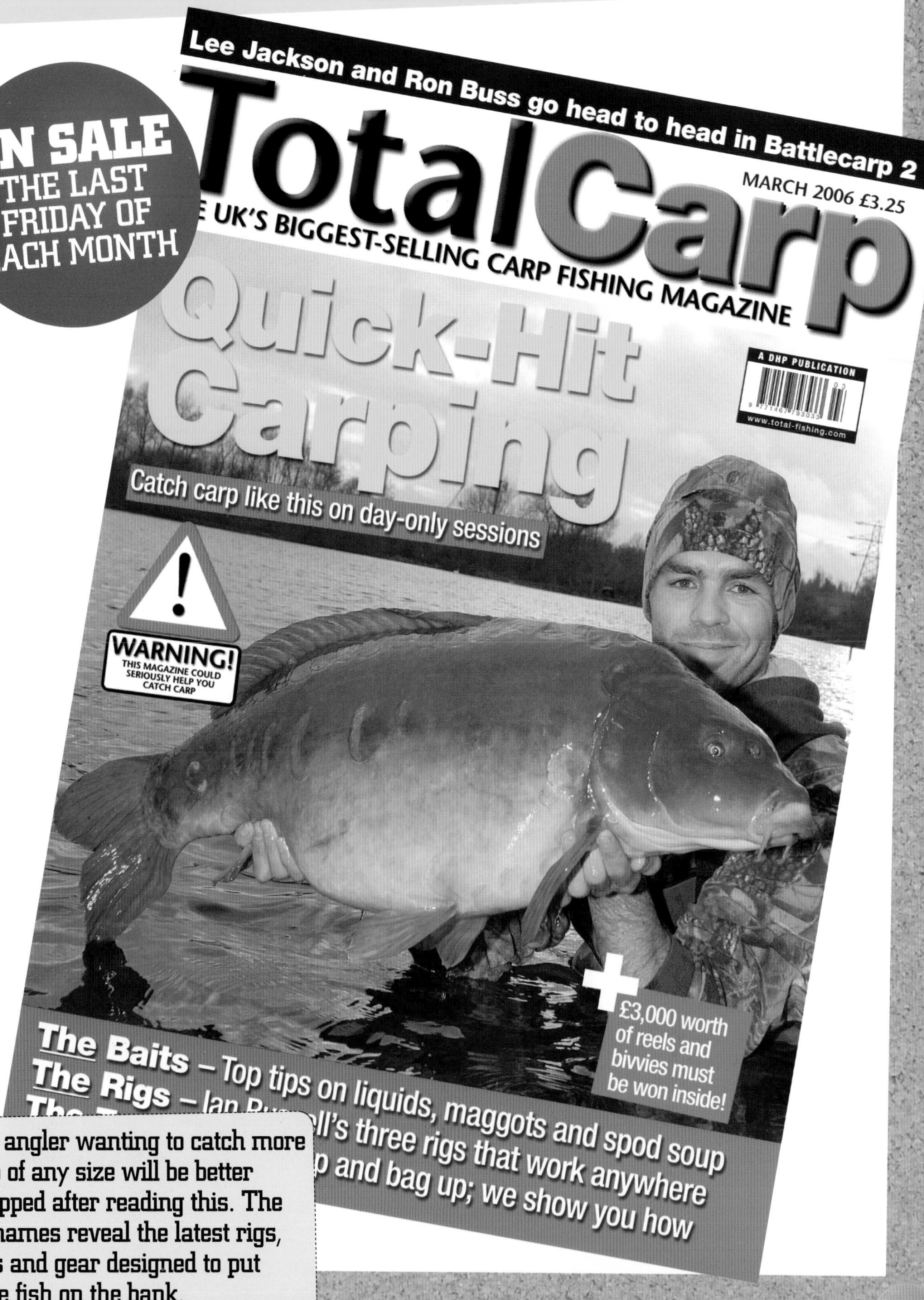
Lee Jackson and Ron Buss go head to head in Battlecarp 2
Total Carp
MARCH 2006 £3.25
E UK'S BIGGEST-SELLING CARP FISHING MAGAZINE
A DHP PUBLICATION
www.total-fishing.com
Quick-Hit Carping
Catch carp like this on day-only sessions
WARNING!
THIS MAGAZINE COULD SERIOUSLY HELP YOU CATCH CARP
£3,000 worth of reels and bivvies must be won inside!
The Baits – Top tips on liquids, maggots and spod soup
The Rigs – Ian R…ll's three rigs that work anywhere
…p and bag up; we show you how

Any angler wanting to catch more carp of any size will be better equipped after reading this. The top names reveal the latest rigs, baits and gear designed to put more fish on the bank.

ANGLER FILE

Name: Neil Smith
Age: 39
UKPB: 34lb 4oz
Nickname: Gerry (Phoenix Nights)
Favourite water: Most northwest waters with carp in!

Going The Distance

Neil Smith reveals 11 distance-fishing tips that will help you cast further. Check 'em out.

Being able to cast a bait a long way is just one of many weapons in a successful carp angler's armoury. While it isn't always necessary to fire a bait to the horizon, occasionally it will turn an otherwise blank session into a productive one.

Distance casting can come into its own on pressured venues, where the carp are used to being caught anywhere from the margins up to about 80yards range. They will learn that feeding within this 'danger zone' can be hazardous and will treat any bait they come across with extreme caution. If you have the ability to put a bait out at range, where the carp aren't used to being caught and feed quite readily, chances are you'll bag up.

Distance casting isn't as difficult as some anglers will have you believe. With a little bit of practice and know-how you'll be casting leads further than ever before. The practice is down to you, but hopefully Neil Smith can help you out with the know-how.

Tip One
Rods & Reels

It is important that the rods and reels you choose for distance fishing are up to the job. It is no good trying to cast over 100 yards with tiny reels and 1.5lb test curve rods.

Neil's choice of weapons are Shimano Tribal LC rods and his new Daiwa Tournament reels. The LC stands for 'long cast' and these rods boast a 3lb test curve. There is plenty of power in the butt of the rod, but the tip is soft enough to protect hook-holds when playing fish at close quarters.

The Tournament reels are big-pit style reels with large-capacity spools that have a very large diameter.

Tip Two
Double Up

When possible, for example when fishing attractor baits at range or boilies over freebies, try fishing with double baits on the hook.

A double-boilie presentation is obviously heavier than a single bait and this helps keep some extra weight forward of the rig and cuts down on tangles.

A short hair, keeping the bait tight to the shank of the hook, can also drastically reduce tangles. Neil normally prefers a slightly longer hair, but it is important to know that your rig is actually 'fishing' and is not sitting in a tangled heap.

Tip Three
Safety First

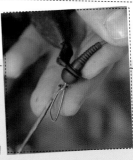

When using a leader of any description it is absolutely crucial that you use a rig that is safe. In the event of a breakage, the carp must be able to rid itself of the rig/lead.

Neil uses running rigs from Fox and Korda, as the large-bore rings will always pass over a leader knot in the event of a breakage above the leader.
PLEASE DO TAKE THIS TIP VERY SERIOUSLY.

Tip Four
Follow My Lead

It is essential to choose the right shape lead for the job, according to Neil. Small, light, dumpy-style leads are no good for distance casting as they are just not aerodynamic.

It is better that the weight is at the front of the lead as it flies, so bomb-shaped and zipp-style leads are best. Neil prefers the Tournament Casting leads from Korda and tends to use a 3oz version for most of his range work but will up the size in sidewinds and where necessary.

Tip Five
A New Breed

Although now very popular, the hybrid hook-link materials are relatively new in the scheme of things. Kryston first launched such hook-link materials as Snake-Skin and then Snake-Bite, before all the current companies developed their own. These days the favourites seem to be Mantis, Stealth Skin and one or two others.

These hooklengths are Neil's first choice when distance fishing as the stiff boom sections improve the rig's anti-tangle properties by keeping the rig away from the lead for as long as possible. The supple inner braids still allow some versatility in these long-range rigs.

In serious headwinds and tricky conditions a straight stiff rig, using something like stiff fluorocarbon such as Grand Max Riverge would be a safer choice.

Tip Six
Perfect PVA

If you are fishing PVA bags, and any such bag will cut down on distance, use them as small and compact as possible. A tiny amount of pellets can be used in a small bag or some groundbait can be formed into a very small 'stick'.

Neil's preference is to crush down a 20mm or 18mm boilie and use the crumb in a tiny PVA bag. The bag is then hooked on to the rig before casting out. The smaller and tighter the bag, the further the cast will go.

Neil's Distance PVA Bag

1 Neil uses mesh-type PVAs with very small holes in, such as these.

2 It is surprising how much crumb can be produced from one 18mm boilie.

3 The single crumbed, 18mm boilie is dropped into the PVA loading system...

4 ... before being tightly compressed into the PVA with a plunger.

5 The plunger is used to push the crumbed boilie out of the end of the loading tube.

6 Neil then ties the bag off as tightly as possible with a simple granny knot.

7 The bag is then trimmed as close to the knot as possible - just the job for distance fishing.

8 This is the size of bag compared to the original, 18mm boilie. There's not much difference.

Tip Seven
Lines & Leaders

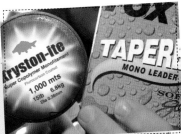

For exceptional casting, a thin diameter main line is an advantage. The thinner the line the lower the breaking strain so it is important to be very careful indeed. Do not try and cast big leads with light main lines without the use of a leader.

Neil is experimenting with some new Krystonite main line from Kryston and he is very excited about it as it offers a combination of a low diameter, strength and abrasion resistance. Although Neil sometimes uses a fluorocarbon main line, fluorocarbon is very heavy and is not suited to casting.

Stick to the monofilament leader materials, preferably the tapered varieties. Neil's favourite is the Fox Tapered Leader material and there is even a diagram included in the pack describing a suitable leader knot and how to tie it safely.

It is important that, before casting, the leader knot is at the bottom of the reel's spool, preventing it from catching on the line as it leaves the reel on the cast.

Tip Ten
Gently, Gently

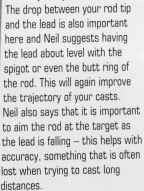

It is important to try and get the rig to straighten as it hits the water so that it doesn't tangle and sits nice and straight on the lake bed.

This can be easily achieved by feathering the line gently as the lead is about to touch down by using your index finger pressed lightly against the lip of the spool.

This, and many of these tips, can be improved greatly with practice – perhaps the very best tip of them all.

Tip Eleven
Aim High

The technique of the cast is very important and if Neil could give one tip it would be to aim high.

Instead of aiming at the point on the water you want to cast to, pick out a point above that area, such as a tree or anything not likely to move, and aim at that. This improves the

trajectory of the cast and will instantly add yards.

The drop between your rod tip and the lead is also important here and Neil suggests having the lead about level with the spigot or even the butt ring of the rod. This will again improve the trajectory of your casts.

Neil also says that it is important to aim the rod at the target as the lead is falling – this helps with accuracy, something that is often lost when trying to cast long distances.

Tip Eight
Tubing

If you are using tubing above the lead as Neil does, for both anti-tangle and fish-safety purposes, only use as much as you need.

If you use just a bit more than the length of your rig this will stop the rig tangling on the main line on the cast. This length of tubing will be sufficient to protect the fish's flanks – too much tubing adds excess weight and will cut down on the distance you'll achieve.

Tip Nine
Play Detective

Bite detection is vital, especially when fishing at range. Because Neil doesn't like fishing with braid, he has to set up his indicators as best he can with the mono main line.

Most bites at range will be drop-backs so Neil fishes with his bobbins right up to the buzzers on tight lines. The heavier the bobbins the better, as these will register the slightest movement.

Neil has used quivers in the past but they kept breaking on the central boss of his pod every time he got a bite and the quiver sprang back down.

Because of the tight lines, Neil is keen not to allow any sound to travel down the line to the area he is fishing. He has recently tried a system from Specialist Tackle that allows him to convert his alarms to cordless remotes. This way he can hear a bleep at the receiver but no noise travels from the alarm down the line.

AT LOVELY COMMON CAUGHT WHILE FISHING AT RANGE.

Mastermind

Dave Lane, one of the country's best carp anglers, answers questions on all things carpy.

This will spell disaster on the cast.

Q How do you prevent your main line from wrapping around the butt eye on the cast, resulting in a crack-off?

A Main line wrapping around the butt ring, or 'frapping' as I've heard it called, is quite a common thing really. It always ends in disaster, too, because your terminal tackle heads off into the distance with an almighty crack. In fact, it happened to me while we were actually shooting the photos to go with these questions!

The most common cause is incorrect tension on the last few yards of line on the spool and this is usually down to loose coils forming before the cast. These coils can occur while you are baiting your rig or just generally moving the rod about while you're on the bank.

To try and alleviate it, just flick the lead out a few yards underarm before casting and wind back in with the line under tension, trapped between your thumb and forefinger. You'll need to position your hand in front of the reel seat to achieve this. This should ensure a tight line loading on the spool and cut down on the problem.

Many anglers I see out on the bank seem to have a particular weight that they use at all times. However, it sometimes pays to be a bit more flexible with the size of lead you choose. By suiting the lead to the situation, that is, using a lighter lead when casting close in, you can use the action of the rod to your advantage.

Doing this will guarantee less problems on the cast, less crack-offs and a considerable saving on lost end tackle.

Build your casting confidence and you'll be able to cast further.

Marker Float

Get the basics right and you'll be well on the way to catching more carp...

The marker rod is a vital piece of equipment for many carp anglers and can be essential for locating likely feeding areas.

While a semi-stiff 2.75lb test curve carp rod will do the job, dedicated marker rods are available and, in our experiences, can be a better bet. If you are going to buy an extra rod for use as a plumbing rod, then you might as well buy one that has been designed with that job in mind. However, if you already have a 'spare' 2.75lb rod, then carry on!

One item of tackle that we definitely recommend you use is braided main line. Because braid does not stretch, it will transmit more information from the lead back to your rod and hands than monofilament will.

There are absolutely loads of marker floats out there, all of which do their job. If you are fishing weedy waters, you'll need a very buoyant float, which will usually have a dumpy body. For clear water, any will suffice. If you are marking up at range, then opt for a float

with a slim, aerodynamic body.

Several companies now manufacture special leads for plumbing, which feature knobbles on them. These act to 'feel' the lake bed better and can even bring back bits of debris from the bottom, giving you an idea of what's out there. To be fair, most leads will do a job. Distance leads fly further, but can also skim over features too easily, whereas more rounded, dumpy leads do not cast as far but give a truer reading of the lake bed.

1

You can use a Free Spirit Searcher kit. Start by attaching the lead to the quick-change clip.

2

Then, trim the silicone tubing to the correct length. It should cover the whole clip.

3

Thread the running ring onto the clip. These rings run very smoothly on the line.

4

Now pull the silicone over the clip and onto the ring. This helps to avoid tangles.

5

Next, thread the main line through the running ring on your Searcher marker kit.

6

Using a baiting needle, thread the cork ball in the kit onto the main line.

7

This cork ball acts as a buffer between the ring and the float. It's also buoyant, which helps.

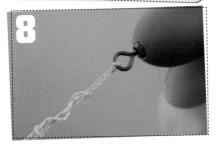

8

After the cork ball, tie on your chosen marker float at the end of the main line.

9

Trim the main line neatly and it's job done! Use braid for marking as it transmits 'feel' better.

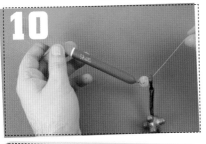

10

This is how the set-up sits on the bottom. Let out the line a foot at a time to find the depth.

Summer Sizzlers

Jason Cann reveals some top tips, guaranteed to get you more bites through summer.

"Summer is a great time to be out on the bank," says Jason Cann. "The weather's warm and there are plenty of fish to be caught. However, there are thousands of anglers who sit behind their rods, catch a couple of fish in a day and are quite pleased with themselves. While there's nothing wrong with that, they could be missing out on the best day's sport they've ever had.

"The deal with the summer months is the same as all year round. By applying a little bit of thought and effort to your angling your catch rate will soar."

There are few better demonstrators of this than Jason. He works extremely hard at his angling and is handsomely rewarded with his catches.

ANGLER FILE

Name: Jason Cann
Age: 31
Occupation: Angling photojournalist
UK PB: 43lb

Tip One
Quality Food Baits

Carp will often get their heads down and feed hard in the summer, especially once they've finished spawning.

Try fishing over a big bed of quality bait. The carp know what's good for them and are much more likely to feed over a bed of top-quality boilies than a bed of cheap pellets or particles, especially if big beds of boilies aren't a common tactic on your water.

Tip Two
Size Matters

Feed a variety of sizes of bait into your swim. This will stop the carp getting used to one particular size and shape of bait. As different-sized baits behave differently in the carp's mouth, it will make your hook bait much harder to identify and more likely to be picked up.

Tip Three
Glugs And Oils

Glugs, dips, bait soaks and oils are all great for adding to your mixers. Not only do they put masses of attraction into your swim, which can be smelt by fish all over the lake, they also create flat spots. By baiting up with oily mixers it will 'kill' any ripple in your swim, making it flat calm and much easier to spot taking fish.

Tip Four
Artificial Baits

These have all sorts of uses but are great surface baits. They never sink, can be easily hooked, take on flavours and additives and never come off the hook. What's more, the corn, pellets, tigers and the like are rarely used on the surface.

Tip Five
Think Big

On occasions it can take hours of continual feeding before the carp start taking off the top. Similarly, if the fish really start 'having it' then you need to give it to them. It's no good taking a little box of mixers because you'll run out almost before you've even begun. You can pick up 15kg sacks of mixers like this one from pet-food suppliers for next to nothing. This sack cost just £6 and Jason used the whole lot in one session.

Tip Six
Spot The Ball

One of the most common problems with surface fishing is that you easily lose sight of your hook bait. You start watching one of the freebies under the impression that it contains your hook and strike when it's taken, spooking the fish.

To prevent this, Jason sticks a little blob of hi-viz floating putty to the top of his hook bait. The result is that he can keep an eye on his bait, even more than 100 yards away.

Tip Seven
Observation

Even though carp are much easier to catch in the summer, if you're not on them, you won't catch. Luckily, the warmer weather will encourage carp to move about and cruise on the top. As a result, they're not too hard to find and therefore target. A decent pair of binoculars, as well as a peaked cap and pair of polarised glasses, will make the fish a lot easier to find.

Tip Eight
Spod God

When the carp get 'on the munch' they can devour mountains of bait in a very short space of time. When this happens you need to 'let them have it' and there is no better way of getting a big bed of bait out at range than a spod (unless boats are allowed, of course).

Jason carries a range of spods with him at all times so that he can cover a variety of situations.

Tip Nine
Location, Location

When trying to locate carp, look in all the usual haunts. Reed beds, lilies, snags, shallow margins and weed beds are all worth checking out.
These are the sorts of areas where the carp will spend the majority of their time and are very catchable when coming and going from these spots. Carp will also give their location away by twitching the reeds and lilies as they swim through them, so keep your eyes peeled.

Tip Ten
Loadsabait

Jason always takes plenty of bait with him in the summer and leaves it in his car. This allows him to be prepared, without having to carry loads of gear.

He has baits to cover all situations and enough of each to bait up heavily if the carp start feeding. This way, Jason can give the carp exactly what they want, when they want it. If you do this you must remember to store any freezer baits, or maggots, worms, casters and suchlike, in a cool bag with a couple of ice packs. Otherwise, it gets messy!

Tip Eleven
Up And Away

It has been said time and time again, but staying mobile is a huge advantage. Carp move about an awful lot in the summer and you have to be prepared to follow them if you want to keep catching. Jason followed the carp down the entire length of the lake during this feature and ended up at the opposite end to where he started, but it paid off.

Tip Twelve
Ooh, My Favourite!

Jason's favourite summer baits are maize, sweetcorn and artificial corn. Maize and sweetcorn have been used for many years and carp still pick it up – they just love the stuff. Used in small quantities, maize and sweetcorn are devastating baits.
To avoid nuisance fish, Jason uses fake corn as a hook bait as it won't come off no matter how much the small fish pull it about.

Tip Thirteen
Pest Control

If small fish become a nuisance and start ripping your hook bait to pieces, try using nuts. Jason rates tiger nuts and peanuts very highly. They withstand nuisance fish for a bit longer than boilies or maize and carp absolutely love them.

You must make sure that nuts are allowed on your water and that they are correctly prepared. If you're not sure how to prepare them properly then buy some of the ready-to-use varieties from your local tackle shop.

Tip Fourteen
Weird And Wonderful

This is the ideal time to play around with baits and rigs that are slightly out of the ordinary. As bites aren't usually hard to come by, you can quickly gauge whether your new tactics are working and fine-tune bait mixes or rigs.

"I love experimenting with odd baits at this time of year," says Jason. "Playing around with my baits and mixes has allowed me to gain an edge over other anglers on the lakes I fish and I know that nobody else is using the same bait, because only I know what's in it."

Ten Top Tips

Expert carp catcher Jon 'Shoes' Jones' 10 edges that will help you catch more carp.

I was a bit concerned that much of what I was doing for this feature was pretty well run-of-the-mill stuff. You see, carp fishing is not as scientific as some people like to make out and many of the best tips are the simplest ones.

However, I am the sort of carp angler that does like to tinker with a few things and so I thought I'd show you some of the little bits and bobs that I am currently playing around with. Now, this is not one of those features where I tell you what you must do in order to catch. No, instead it simply outlines some of the tricks that I am employing at the moment, a few of which are still very much at the experimental stage. Hopefully, there are one or two things outlined here that will be relevant to you. So why not give them a go and see if they work for you? They may help you catch the fish of a lifetime.

Tip One
Hiding The End Tackle

I use a lot of looped Snide leaders from Berkley. These leaders come in different lengths and colours. The colours match different lake beds, from sandy ones to thick, black, silty ones. On gravel I use a clear leader but, for the more camou-minded angler out there, try marking your leader/tubing with a permanent marker pen. The ones I have are from a local stationery store.

Tip Two
Camou Groundbait?

We have all used groundbaits at some stage in our fishing career. Some have been fantastic, while others didn't seem to do any good. Why? Well, sorry, I don't know the answer to that. But have you thought it may have been down to the colour? Imagine you're on a very-well-stocked water where there's a good chance of a few carp on each session. You would be looking to get as many takes as you can, so you might use a visual groundbait. On the flip side, you might be fishing for some old wary carp and the visual approach may not work. This is when you might try and match the colour of the groundbait to the colour of the lake bed.

I am more confident fishing for bigger carp with a dark groundbait, such as Swimstim Amino Black.

Tip Three
Spod And Bag Mixes

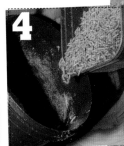

Spodding has become the norm for everyone nowadays, but how many of you use the same spod/PVA bag mix? What I'm trying to say is that your bag mix should be as close as possible to the mix you're spodding out. The biggest problem is that your spod mix could be wet… and we all know what happens with wet mixes in PVA bags!

I like to use very similar ingredients in both my spod and bag mixes, just so there isn't any change in colour or texture which might otherwise cause the carp to expect danger. I like to use natural ingredients, such as maggots, worms, bloodworm and shrimps – all these are used for both bag and spod mixes.

The spod mix in its standard form will be wet, so it will not be suitable as a bag mix. But by adding some oil the contents will have a coating to prevent the bag from melting on the cast or while in midair.

How many times has your PVA stocking come off on the cast? A few, I'll bet! Simply add a small amount of oil to the dry spod mix in a small container or maggot box. Lightly cover the mix and stir it well – this should coat it with a PVA-friendly film and, in turn, lets you fish with bait exactly the same as your spod mix. The only thing that needs to be changed from time to time is your hook bait, again in size and in colour.

First, add a simple bag mix or groundbait to an empty bucket.

Follow this with a couple of handfuls of pellets. Try and use a variety of sizes.

Bloodworm is the next ingredient. Carp go crazy for this stuff.

Next, add a pint of maggots. No carp can resist maggots.

Pour in your chosen oil or glug. Mix everything together thoroughly.

Make sure the entire mix is the same consistency and, ideally, slightly damp.

To darken it down, mix in some Swimstim Amino Black groundbait.

There you have it, a bait that can be spodded out or used in PVA bags.

Tip Four
Boom Or Bust!

Adding a boom on my marker float set-up has helped keep the marker float out of the way of any silkweed, which can snag up in the ring and prevent the float from rising. You must remember to add the length of the boom to any depths found when plumbing.

However, if the float rises we assume that it's clear on the bottom, don't we? That may not be true when using a boom. I would say that if you use a boom currently, then try plumbing the same spots without one. The results might surprise you and will give you a clearer picture of what's out there.

Tip Five
Shine A Light

Being involved in the British Carp Angling Championship, I have seen lots of carp anglers experiencing the same problem: baiting up and casting back to the same spot in the dark!

I have come across a very good way of helping me to see my marker float and to find the mark on my line. Turning up on a Friday night after work, especially in winter, means having to bait up, cast out and set up in the dark. I can almost guarantee that some things will go astray.

This is where my mate John Finch from Bankside Tackle came to my rescue. He gave me some glow-in-the-dark adhesive tape and some reflective tape and this has helped me no end. Sticking it onto my marker float and spod has helped me bait up in the dark. It glows long enough to put a bit of bait out and, with the extra bit of reflective tape, I can see my float with a torch.

Tip Six
Stay Sharp

Since I have been carp fishing I have never found a set of blades that will cut braid with ease, until now! It is important to have the best equipment you can afford. Fly fishermen who tie their own flies will use a quality set of blades. Why do we as carp anglers use a cheaper alternative when we too tie our own rigs and so on? In the past I have used cheap blades that wouldn't cut braid at the first attempt. It's frustrating and I end up burning the tag end to make it neater.

Owner has come up with a set of blades that, without doubt, have made rig tying, especially with braid, far easier. At around 12 quid they may seem a bit expensive, but compared to the ones from fly fishing shops they are a snip (excuse the pun).

Tip Seven
Back To Braid

I feel that braided hook links will go full circle and we will be using them again for most of our fishing. I still use a coated hook link but only for single-bait fishing. I have been tying rigs made from braid for a while and have found that they are more versatile and flexible.

They are more suited to PVA-bag fishing and are more effective in short lengths. Many anglers have used the PVA-stick method with a coated hook link. Depending on which hook link you are using, I would say it will float and lift up from the lake bed, forming a loop from bait to lead after the PVA has melted. To prevent this you need to apply a couple of tungsten blobs to ensure that the hook link sinks. Now, threading this through the PVA will cause the tungsten blobs to slide down the link and not where you want them to be. By using braid with a 'rub' of tungsten along its length, the problem is alleviated.

The hook link will stay rooted to the lake bed and not looped up above the groundbait. I cannot stress enough that this is my finding and I'm not suggesting that you should stop using your favourite hook-link material. But, from what I have seen when filming underwater, a short braided rig performed better than, say, an 8in coated hook link. The carp can, surprisingly, get away with a lot of things, but I feel that we give them too much credit. There's no doubt that carp get caught on 'looped-up' combi-rigs, but I also feel that plenty more get away with it with the same presentation.

Tip Eight
Open Wide

Choosing the right hooks can be more frustrating than fishing. There are so many out there these days that settling on just one or two patterns can be nigh-on impossible for many carp anglers. During the last few winters I have been using long-shanked hooks, but recently I have been using short, wide-gaped hooks.

Firstly, I would look for a hook that will suit the bait I want to use. If I'm using bait that's small I would like to use a hook that's also small. I wouldn't look for a long-shanked hook if I was using a small, 10mm bait for example. I have found that a small, wide-gaped hook holds better when used with small bait. It might be worth playing around with hook shape and size to match the bait you're using. By fine-tuning your hook you could just put a couple more on the bank.

Tip Nine
Trim Up!

Baits come in all different shapes and sizes, from a grain of hemp to a big cube of luncheon meat. We all use these baits straight from the packet or tin. Let's recap slightly. We all use these baits. Yes we do, and with a great deal of success. A round boilie is always a round boilie. A barrel-shaped trout pellet is always a barrel-shaped trout pellet. Can you see what I'm getting at?

I mentioned earlier about colour, now what about the shape. Start playing around with the shape of the things. All these baits will keep catching fish and by playing around with

the shape you could be putting a few extra carp on the bank. That's why bait companies produce pellet-shaped boilies that are just the same as the round version but, because they're a different shape, they fool the carp into thinking they're something else.

Tip Ten
Quiet Please

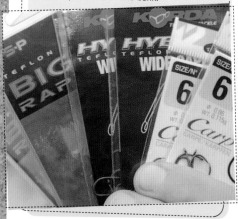

On a personal level, I love alarms with a remote system. Why? Well, it's not because I can go around to my mate's swim and leave my rods out. It's down to the sound level. I like to have no sound at all coming from the alarm head. Even if I'm only feet away from my rods, I still use the remote with the volume down very low. This is for two reasons. Firstly, I like to keep my swim quiet and I don't want to give away the fact that I'm catching. When fishing a day ticket water, the last thing I want is anglers moving in next door and trying to fish as close to me as they can because I'm catching. Your alarms are the biggest giveaway of any action.

Secondly, we found while filming the Carp Show that the sounds/vibrations would travel down the line and could be detected by carp. We could be frightening them just by having our alarms sounding.

ANGLER FILE

Name: Lee Jackson
Age: 49
Occupation: Carp fishing consultant
UK PB: 61lb 7oz

Jacko's Winter Tips

When it's cold out there, bites will be hard to come by so we asked carp-catching ace Lee Jackson to show you 13 ways to catch more carp in winter.

Tip One
Venue Choice

A great deal of winter success is down to choosing the right venue. Pick a well-stocked water that continues to be fished by other anglers throughout the colder months. Regular introduction of bait should keep carp searching for food and the disturbance anglers create should keep the fish moving about regularly.

Tip Two
Winter Winners

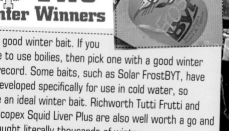

Select good winter bait. If you choose to use boilies, then pick one with a good winter track record. Some baits, such as Solar FrostBYT, have been developed specifically for use in cold water, so they're an ideal winter bait. Richworth Tutti Frutti and Nash Scopex Squid Liver Plus are also well worth a go and have caught literally thousands of winter carp.

Tip Three
Au Naturel

Natural baits catch carp all year round, but they really come into their own in the winter. A bunch of maggots on the hook coupled with a PVA bag of the little wrigglers will get you plenty of bites. Most people seem to use red maggots, but I've had a lot of success with white, or natural-coloured, ones. You can present them on a rig ring, on a hair, or simply place them on the hook. Give them a go.

Tip **Four**
Fine It Down

Fine down your end tackle. There's no need to take things to the extreme, but a size 8 or 10 hook with an 8lb or 10lb mono hooklength is all you need for winter success. Keep your rigs simple too. Bites can be few and far between, so you don't want to lessen your chances further by using a tangled rig.

Tip **Five**
Eye Spy

A piece of hi-viz artificial corn will add masses of visual attraction to your hook bait. It might just be enough to get an otherwise uninterested carp to pick up your bait.

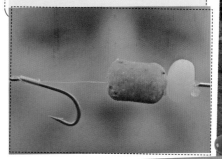

Tip **Six**
Hide And Seek

Don't ignore any visual signs that might be caused by carp. Swirls, bubbling, crashing fish and head and shouldering will all tell you where the carp are hiding and are well worth casting at. Sometimes bubbling can be caused by gasses rising from the lake bed, but if you're unsure then cast at it; it might just have been caused by a carp.

Tip **Seven**
Small Mouthfuls

Don't use masses of bait. Tiny PVA bags filled with small food items such as 3mm pellets are all you need. Nine times out of 10 in winter, carp will eat a small mouthful of food and ignore a big bed of bait. Because of the cold temeratures their bodies cannot cope with vast amounts of food.

Tip **Eight**
The Singles Game

Hi-attract, single-hook baits work in the cold. Use bright-coloured baits and recast them regularly until you find the carp. On heavily stocked waters, single pieces of hi-viz artificial corn work well – I can't explain why, they just do

Tip Nine
Indication

Use a sensitive indication set-up. Lightweight bobbins and slack lines are my choice. It also helps if the sensitivity on your alarms can be adjusted. Don't always expect screaming runs in winter, a few bleeps might be the only indications you get. Using running rigs will also improve your bite indication because they're extremely sensitive.

Tip Ten
Keep A Record

Take notes. Keep a record of where and when you catch a winter carp. These notes will enable you to locate hotspots and bite times that'll lead to you being a more efficient and successful winter angler. The more information you can record, the better.

11-15am Lost fish
Left Hand Rod, 40 yard toward
left hand white post on far bank

11-45am 14lb Mirror
Middle rod 40 yards slightly right
of left hand white post on far bank

Tip Eleven
Stay Warm

This tip isn't directly related to fishing, but it is related to your comfort while on the bank. This might sound a little strange, but when you're sitting waiting for a bite rest your feet on your unhooking mat. The extra insulation it provides will keep your feet warmer than if they're resting on the ground. A cold angler won't be concentrating on catching a carp.

Tip Twelve
If All Else Fails

If all else fails, try these – Solar's Jacko Pops. They are made from a recipe I was using for years, way before I gave it to Solar, and I have enjoyed massive success with these at all times of year.

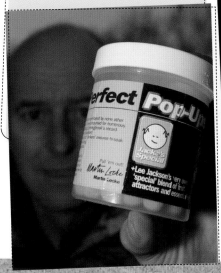

Tip Thirteen
Don't Be Afraid Of The Dark

Time is limited on day sessions in winter, so make the most of the time you have. Get to the water at first light, if not before, and fish through until it gets dark. By spending an extra hour or so by the water you might just nick an extra bite in the dark.

IF YOU'RE GOING TO PUT YOUR RELATIONSHIP ON THE LINE, AT LEAST HAVE A THREESOME.

She's not going to like it! But after you've cranked the handle on the latest Tournament Basia, she's going to have to lump it.

The new Basia carries the highly acclaimed Tournament name to the next level in carp reels. An incredibly light, 45mm long, anodised spool, crossed with immaculate line lay makes the Basia one of, if not the ultimate casting reel around.

But distance is only part of the game. To help you with the rest the Basia incorporates a new, superb 'Quick Drag'. This offers the perfect cross-over from front drag to free spool without the need for conversions, giving you precise control at critical moments.

We've also added neat touches like drilled Isotope holes on the spool skirt which allows you to identify the running reel at night much quicker. A custom designed line clip, infinite anti-reverse, stainless steel AirBail, Cast Lock, machined one piece alloy handle and the trade mark wooden knob. All held together by a super light magnesium alloy body.

So just imagine 3 of these babies locked onto your rods and ready for action. The new Basia. The reel that's worth getting nagged over.

ULTRA LIGHT DESIGN **QUICK DRAG SYSTEM** **TOURNAMENT LINE CLIP** **ISOTOPE HOLES**

Model	Ratio	Weight Ozs	BB	Line Capacity	RRP
BAS45QDA	4.1:1	17.8	7	240m-12lb	£375

The world's biggest specialist.

Daiwa
COMMITTED TO TOTAL QUALITY

daiwasports.co.uk

Undercover Carping

Get down to your local pond, be stealthy and catch carp under the rod tip...

A low-twenty, stalked under the rod tip – beltin'!

ANGLER FILE

Name: Marc Coulson
Age: 33
Occupation: Editor, Total Carp
Favourite water: Hunt's Corner, Linear Fisheries

If I was made to choose only one form of carp fishing, that choice would have to be stalking.

The thrill of actually watching a carp at close quarters and seeing it approach and then, hopefully, take your hook bait is second to none.

There is so much more to carp fishing than simply sitting behind three rods on a pod, in the same swim, for your entire session. Give me my bucket, stalking rod, landing net and unhooking mat over that any day.

Stalking needn't be rocket science either. I have had a few readers of Total Carp say to me on the bank that they don't bother stalking because it looks too tricky. This misconception could not be further from the truth and there are a lot of things that you can do to make it very easy indeed.

There's loads of gear available for the stalking angler, too. However, apart from a few bits that I would recommend you try and get, you do not need to make wholesale changes to your gear.

One of the great things about stalking is the whole mobility thing. Being able to turn up at a lake, armed only with a few bits of tackle and then roam around freely is great, especially if you do not have loads of time on your hands.

I often keep a bit of stalking kit in the car so I can make the most of any opportune chance to go fishing after work, especially in summer.

So, how should you approach a bit of stalking? Well, the first thing I would say is that you need to choose the right water. By this, I do not mean that stalking does not work everywhere, but some fisheries insist that you only fish from designated swims. You can still catch carp at short range here, especially late in the day, but you do not have the option to roam around looking for margin feeders.

Let's assume, then, that the water you are on does allow a bit of stalking. The first thing to do is walk around the lake and find some likely looking spots to fish.

The anticipation as fish enter the swim is heart stopping.

By watching the water, in particular the margins, you will eventually find areas that fish frequent or travel through.

Carp are creatures of habit and will often patrol the margins, particularly when the fishery is quiet. These patrolling carp are the easiest to target.

If I find an area that carp are passing through, I will see it as a potential ambush spot. By introducing a few handfuls of bait, usually pellets, I can wait and see whether or not the carp will stop on the bait when they return. If they do, I have a chance of catching them.

TRY AND BAIT UP AT LEAST THREE OR FOUR LIKELY LOOKING SPOTS.

Don't be in a hurry to fish for these carp. Let them leave the area, then add some more bait for when they return. If they eat the bait again, then repeat this a third time, but this time introduce your baited rig.

I have sat for hours just feeding fish I have spotted in the margins until they were confident. Ideally, you want more than one fish competing for the bait. This way the carp are more likely to make a mistake and get hooked when you introduce your rig.

There are always occasions when this

Travel light – this is as much as you need to take when stalking.

Put your keys away and turn your phone to silent – or you risk spooking the carp.

Paste and boilies – Marc's favoured stalking combination.

Wrap the paste around your hook...

... but leave the hook point exposed.

may not work as explained, but generally this is the best way to stalk carp. I once went stalking and found a single fish in the margins. After introducing individual, broken boilies, the fish was tempted to eat the odd one, before starting to really munch on them. As soon as the carp 'turned its back' I gently lowered a freelined paste hook bait down into the edge. The fish returned, ate a few more boilies and then snaffled my hook bait. Five minutes later I had a low-twenty on the bank.

Don't put all your eggs in one basket, though. If you can, and there aren't too many other anglers on the lake who might take advantage, try and bait up at least three or four likely looking spots. If for any reason you cannot catch from your first spot, then you'll have another already baited up and ready to go.

Wander around the lake after feeding these areas and look for signs of carp activity. If the water is not clear enough that you can actually see the carp, there may still be signs of them being there.

There are many ways of telling if carp are, or have been, present. Look for cloudiness in the water – a sure sign that the bottom has been disturbed, usually by carp eating your freebies. Also, you might spot creases on the water surface or even a rocking of the water as those big old fins and tails create disturbance.

In terms of actually fishing for the carp, I have three favourite methods. The first one is to use a standard carp set-up. By this I mean my favoured rig that I'd regularly use for my 'normal' carp fishing. I use this rig when the water is very coloured, with depths that I am unsure of, and also when I do not know what the lake bed consists of. I don't want to drop a freelined piece of paste into a margin that I do not know the make-up of, for instance. It could land in a big pile of weed and be rendered useless.

The second, and more traditional tactic, is float fishing. My rig is simplicity itself, and combines a clear waggler with a small weight and a braid hook link.

The last, and my favourite, way of stalking is simply freelining. Freelining means exactly that – there are no floats, leads or anything else attached to the line; just the hook and your bait. I use all sorts of baits for this, including corn, worms, meat, bread and paste. The paste method is a particular favourite and works extremely well.

I have a neat little trick that I use to great effect when fishing paste. I use a paste that matches my usual boilie hook baits. What I do is feed boilies that I have squeezed between my fingers until they

Even lines come in camou these days!

Try This Float Rig For Stalking Carp

1

Fluorocarbon main line is great for stalking – try 6lb or 8lb. You'll also need to use very sharp hooks as there is no heavy lead.

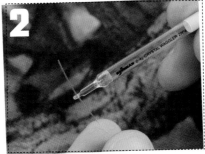

2

I start by using the smallest float I can get away with and thread the main line through the eye, like so.

3

Next, I trim a short piece of silicone tubing and thread this on to the main line, below the float.

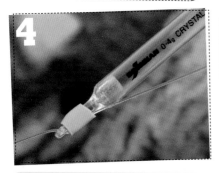

4

The tubing is pulled onto the bottom of the float. This will secure the float without the need for split shot or the like.

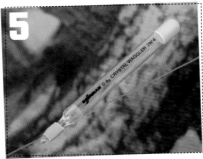

5

With the float attached to the main line like this I can easily slide it up and down to the correct depth.

6

I now tie the end of the main line onto the large ring of a size eight Korda Ring Swivel. These have a nice dull finish.

7

Next, I take a 12in section of braid and tie the hook to it, using a knotless knot or palomar knot (see pages 82 to 83).

8

Once the hook is tied on, I am left with eight inches or so of the braid. This is the supple hook link for the float rig.

9

I then tie this hook link onto the same large ring on the swivel. I favour a grinner or palomar knot for this.

10

Once the tag ends of the two knots are trimmed, the rig will look like this, with the swivel hanging freely between the two lines.

11

I then use some Kryston Heavy Metal rig putty and mould it around the barrel of the swivel, as shown here.

12

The putty cocks the float and helps the hooking potential, acting as a partial bolt rig. That's it, job done!

are like fat discs. I then shape my paste hook bait to resemble these boilies. I have caught loads of fish doing this, so give it a try.

Another great stalking bait is a corn, hemp and pellet combination. The pellets, mixed with hemp and a few grains of corn, really grab the attention of passing carp. The corn is also very visual, so this tactic works in two ways. When fishing over this combination, I usually freeline or float fish three or four grains of side-hooked corn – an absolute winner!

I rarely hair rig my hook baits when stalking. This is because, in many cases, I can see the fish pick up the bait, either literally or via the float. I will then strike rather than hesitate, as you might when waiting for a lead to set the hook.

I am not confident with a hair in these situations, because I feel that fish can often take in the bait and not the hook, due to the different angles involved compared to 'conventional' carp fishing with semi-fixed, bolt-type rigs.

So, what then of the tackle that you need? It's a bit like floater fishing here, in that you can use the gear that you already have, but you may improve your chances if you use a few special bits and pieces.

If you are stalking fish under bushes or overhanging trees, or indeed in tight situations, you will need a short rod. There are loads of stalking rods available from many of the major companies. I have a bit of a collection and have a rod for all situations, but you don't need to go out and start buying three or four stalking rods.

The fish have drifted out of the swim...

... so Marc pops up and flicks his bait out. They'll be back!

Great hooks for stalking with paste.

Stay out of the carp's sight.

Dedicated stalking rods are great fun.

If you buy just one rod, go for something between eight and 10 feet long and a with test curve of around 2.5lb. This will be a good all-rounder.

Don't use big-pit-type reels. You don't need the line capacity, or the excess weight. A small reel will do the job sufficiently, especially given the short-range nature of the fishing.

Other than that, the standard tackle you have will suffice. You will, of course, need some floats if you want to float fish. Small, clear ones are best, especially when fishing clear water.

A small bag of some description will be handy for carrying the small amount of bits you need to take. I put all my baits and stuff in a bucket, which also doubles as a seat! I then use a Chub Bits Belt to keep bits of terminal tackle, floats, my phone and my keys in. On the subject of mobiles, turn your phone off or to silent when stalking – noise scares carp away! Finally, you must be as stealthy as possible and make yourself unnoticable to the carp. This can include getting all camou'd up. There is some great camou stuff out there and you can make yourself really disappear into the background.

You name it and somebody has probably made one in camou. While I am a massive fan of the camou stuff, you don't HAVE to use it. What I will say though, is that strolling along the bank in a bright red, yellow or white T-shirt will not increase your chances when stalking carp.

There is something that I would point out here about the whole camou thing. I have had people say to me that it's

ONE OF MY FAVOURITE CAPTURES EVER – STALKED IN THE EDGE!

Marc Coulson's Stalking Groundbait Mix

1 Hemp and corn is a classic combination – carp love it.

2 Pour some Hinders Mini Combo pellet mix into a tray or bucket.

3 Then add some larger, high-oil Dynamite trout pellets.

4 Marc uses only a little hemp juice, as he wants a dryish mix.

5 The hemp itself then goes into the mix. Hemp is great stuff!

6 Marc then adds sweetcorn and some of the juice.

7 The whole lot is then mixed to combine all the ingredients.

8 Leave the mix for 10 minutes and you're ready to go.

unnecessary and that carp cannot see you anyway. "Camou is just for tackle tarts," some say. In my opinion, it's just like anything else. I ask myself two questions when looking at any carp tackle, bait or accessories, especially new ones: Will it help me catch more carp? Will it cause me to catch less carp? In the case of all the Realtree camou stuff that has made the transition into angling from hunting, it cannot possibly cause you to catch less carp. If there is just a chance that it might help you catch one carp, on one given day, then it's worth it.

I have to admit that it does also look very good, so, yes, it does appeal to the fashion-conscious angler as well.

An obvious extension of the stealthy approach is that you should stay back from the edge of the lake as much as possible. The most likely thing to spook a carp in the margins is movement. You can move around as much as you want, but do it in view of the carp and they'll be off like a shot!

Sadly, you cannot always control what others do. I remember being on a lake at the Linear Fisheries complex, doing a bit of stalking. I had what was then the biggest carp I'd ever seen almost eating corn out of my hand. The next thing I know a big, burly angler came bounding up to me and almost shouted: "What you doing there mate, have you got 'em feeding?"

With more than a hint of anger in my voice, I pointed out how I HAD been trying to stalk a carp, which by now had made its exit. I have never seen that carp again since, except in photographs, and I hopefully won't see the bloke either!

Get out there and try some stalking – you'll love it. Given just one way of catching carp, this would be mine. Plan your trip, find some spots, get the fish feeding and, most of all, have some fun.

Small reels are fine for stalking...

... and a pair of polarising sunglasses are essential.

Mastermind

Dave Lane, one of the country's best carp anglers, answers questions on all things carpy.

Q What are your favourite surface baits and are there any alternative surface baits that you can recommend?

A I suppose my favourite surface bait is mixers, as the fish see so many of them that they just keep on working. The problem is that the carp see that many that it becomes increasingly easier for them to differentiate between the freebies and the hook baits. By mixing the size of the free offerings a bit, you can keep the fish off guard as they have less of a point of reference. I tend to mix small pellets, normal mixers and various cat foods in together to keep a varied feed going in.

Artificial mixers seemed to be the answer to every surface-angler's dreams for a while. They sat up in the water like a real biscuit and kept the hook out of the water, making it harder to see. Unfortunately, the carp are starting to wise up a bit to these on some of the harder-fished waters and it's back to gluing on real ones again. Gluing mixers is a fiddly and time-consuming job but it can be a very productive method. Bread is another favourite of mine, especially a small, square piece of crust from the side of a sliced loaf.

As for alternative baits, cork can be very effective at times. I take a bit of time out before a floater session and make up some small, self-righting, imitation mixers from wine bottle corks. I use a small, bright-yellow square of foam in one side as a hooking point and sight marker. On the other side I glue a tiny pole fishing weight or split shot as a counterbalance. I find that these will work well on waters where the larger rubber imitations are starting to lose their effectiveness.

Pop-ups of 10mm are also one of my favourites, particularly when I am using zig rigs on the surface. Different colours seem to work better on different lakes. Artificial corn has also given me the odd bonus fish, as have brown rubber pellets. On the shelves at Tesco there's a range of dog food products that all are capable of catching fish; it's just a case of sorting out which one floats and which one sinks. You really need a dog at home to steal it from, otherwise it can be a bit expensive!

Another area that I want to explore this summer is fishing with the artificial flies that trout fisherman use. Not by whipping them around my head like J R Hartley and frothing up the water into a foaming mass, but presenting them on a normal controller rig and, maybe, just twitching them across the surface a little bit to give them some life. Some of the patterns are fantastic. I can't wait to try them out.

Alternative Surface Baits

Bait 1
Kryston Doppel-Gänger: it's certainly different, can be moulded to whatever shape you like and it floats!

Bait 2
Dry flies: coupled with a surface controller set-up, these just might work.

Bait 3
Little pop-ups: can be used with a controller set-up, but they're great for surface fishing with zig rigs.

Bait 4
Artifical baits: floating bits of plastic have caught a carp or two. Give them a go, they might work for you too.

Mixers and floating pellets are Dave's favourite surface baits.

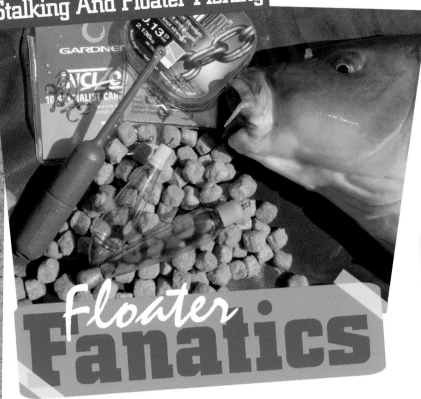

Floater Fanatics

ANGLER FILE

Name: Jon Bones
Nickname: Bonesy
Age: 21
Occupation: Deputy editor, Total Carp
UK PB: 36lb 8oz

ANGLER FILE

Name: Mark Holmes
Nickname: Sherlock
Age: 44
Occupation: Editor, Advanced Carp Fishing
UK PB: 41lb 1oz

Jon Bones and Mark Holmes show you 17 top tips for catching carp off the surface. Why not give them a try...

If you have ever caught a carp off the surface then you will know just how exhilarating it can be. You watch with your heart in your mouth as the carp devours the freebies before delicately taking your hook bait.

If you haven't experienced this yet then you are definitely missing out, and we strongly suggest you try this method.

Like all forms of fishing, though, catching carp off the top can be tricky at times, especially if the carp in your lake have been 'hammered' on floating baits. However, it remains one of the most exciting ways to catch carp.

So take a look at these 17 top tips and see if they can't help you to catch more carp off the top.

Tip One
Glug Your Mixers

Adding a glug or oil to your mixers will flatten any ripple on the surface of the water. This makes it much easier to spot taking fish and keep an eye on your hook bait. It also gives your baits an added boost of attraction.

Tip Two
Colour And Flavour Your Mixers

If the carp in your lake are getting wary of surface baits try adding flavours and colours to them to make them different from anything else they might have seen. Flavours and colourings designed for making boilies are ideal.

Tip Three
Wear Polarising Glasses

It's vital that you can see what's going on in your swim so, if you don't already own a pair, get yourself some decent polarising glasses.

If you don't know which ones to buy check out the Bench Test feature in the August '05 issue of Total Carp.

Tip Four
Use A Floating Main Line And Hooklength

If your line sinks you'll struggle to control your rig and will find striking very difficult. A sinking line will also spook the carp, and a sinking hooklength will drag your hook bait closer to the controller. If your line does sink you can treat it with a line dressing such as Mucilin to make it float.

Tip Five
Feed Your Mixers Upwind Of The Carp

Allow the mixers to drift over the fish. Feeding and casting directly on top of the carp will spook them, causing them to move off. Remember, competition kills caution. Keep the bait going into your swim to get the carp feeding confidently and competing for the food before you cast in.

Tip Six
Use A Soft-Actioned, Purpose-Built Controller Rod

Controller rods have been designed specifically for casting small controllers and playing fish on light lines. If you don't have a purpose-built controller rod, however, a soft-tipped carp rod with a 2lb test curve will do.
Fishing with light lines and small controllers is extremely difficult with a stiff, powerful rod. If you use a rod that's too heavy you're likely to suffer from hook-pulls too.

Tip Seven
Use A Braided Main Line

Line with very little or no stretch will help to set the hook into shy-biting fish, as you are in direct contact with the rig. However, using a braided main line and a light, mono hooklength is a recipe for disaster if you're an inexperienced surface angler.

Tip Eight
Feed A Mixture Of Floating Baits

This gives the carp a variety of sizes, shapes and flavours of baits and stops them getting used to one particular surface bait.

Tip Nine
Watch Your Hook Bait

Too many people watch the controller instead of the bait, but if the carp are feeding cautiously they will eject the bait before they move the controller. You can use a brightly coloured hook bait to make it easier to see.

Tip Ten
Carry A Selection Of Controllers

Use the right one for the situation you're in. For example, there's no need to use a 15g controller if the carp are just 20 yards out, so use the smallest controller you can get away with. Remember, the weight of the controller will also affect how quickly the rig drifts.

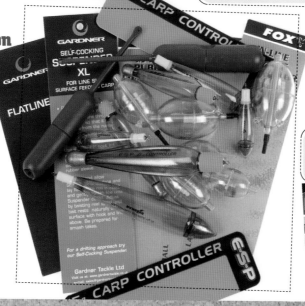

Tip Eleven
Small Hooks Are Ideal For Surface Fishing

Always match the size of the hook to the hook bait. It's no good trying to fish with a single mixer on a size 4 hook.

Tip Twelve
Take Plenty Of Bait

If the carp are really 'having it' then a small box of mixers won't last five minutes. You don't want to have to pack up mid-session because you've run out of bait. However, don't pile loads of bait in at the start of a session, or you could ruin your chances. See how the fish react to a few pouchfuls of mixers, and then gauge how much bait to put in.

Tip Thirteen
Never Cast On Top Of Feeding Fish

To avoid spooking the carp, cast past them and then gently draw the hook bait back to where they are feeding

Tip Fourteen
Prepare Your Hook Baits Before Your Session

If you plan on hooking the mixers it's no good trying to prepare them on the bank, as they take a while to soften.

Presoaking your hook baits in boiling water for a few minutes will do the job but remember to store them separately from your unprepared mixers.

Tip Fifteen
Fill Your Reel Spool To The Brim

Casting light controllers with an under-filled spool is very difficult.

Tip Sixteen
Bait Bands Are A Great Way Of Attaching A Mixer To Your Hook

To ensure the mixer doesn't come off on the cast, place a standard mixer in the band and then leave it in water for a minute. The mixer will swell slightly, making the band grip it more tightly.

Tip Seventeen
Try Using Light Lines For Hooklengths

The fish can sometimes see your hooklength, especially if it's quite thick. Reducing the diameter of your hooklength can sometimes solve the problem. However, never use a line that's so light you cannot safely land what you hook.

FROM HIS TERRACED HOUSE IN THE SLEEPY TOWN OF GRIMSBY THIS MAN STARTED A REVOLUTION.

Rod Hutchinson has forgotten more about carp fishing than you'll ever know. From his ground breaking bait development in 1980 through to the world championship winning Dream Maker rod, the man has a legendary place in our sport.

Some may feel what he has done is enough, but innovation breeds a desire for more success and so Rod has created a new generation of equipment and a new generation of dream makers.

Making dreams come true

Knots

Which knots should you use and how do you tie them? These are popular questions among newcomers to carp fishing. Let's Go Carp Fishing reveals the only four knots you'll ever need...

Poorly tied knots will result in lost fish. If you're at all unsure about tying a reliable knot, then this feature is a must-read for you.

There are so many knots out there that it's easy to become confused. There are knots with twists, turns, loops and tucks, but how do you tie them and what are they all for?

The way to approach the subject of knots is to keep it simple. Although there are literally dozens of knots to choose from, the reality is that by mastering just a few of them you'll have enough ammunition to tie safe, effective rigs.

The four knots we've highlighted in this feature will cover 99.9 per cent of the situations you're likely to find yourself in. The knots – palomar, grinner, knotless and perfect loop – are all strong, simple to tie and extremely reliable when tied correctly. If you struggle to tie these knots, or are just a little unsure, take a bit of time to perfect them – it'll be well worth it in the long run.

A little tip for tying knots, especially when using monofilament, is to moisten the knot with a bit of saliva before tightening it. This will reduce the friction created when it is tightened down, thereby reducing damage to the mono and avoiding weakening the knot.

How To Tie The Palomar Knot

1

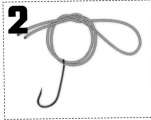
2

3

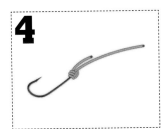
4

The palomar knot is extremely strong and easy to tie. It originated from sea fishing and is ideal for attaching swivels to hooklengths or tying hooks when a hair is not required. This is a real favourite of top carp angler Derek 'The Don' Ritchie and he uses it almost exclusively.

The Grinner Knot – Get It Right

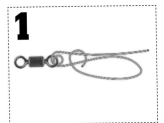
1

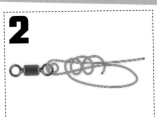
2

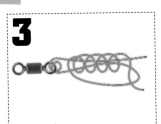
3

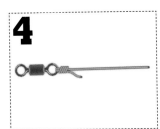
4

The grinner is an alternative to the palomar and is often written about in carp fishing. It's ideal for attaching swivels. The grinner can be tied with monofilament or braided lines, but should not be used with stiff rig materials as it can be very tricky to get right and can cause the line to kink.

The Popular Knotless Knot

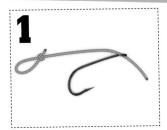
1

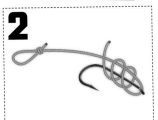
2

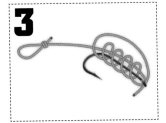
3

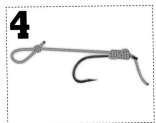
4

The knotless knot forms the basis of most modern carp rigs. It's ultra-effective, strong, reliable and accounts for thousands of carp captures each year. If you only learn to tie one knot when you start carping, make sure it's this one. It is equally good when tied with monofilament or braided lines.

Tie The Perfect Loop Knot

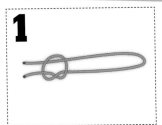
1

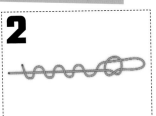
2

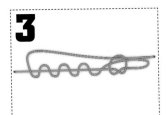
3

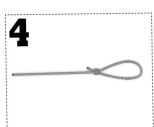
4

This knot will give you a perfect loop every time. Many top carp anglers choose this style of loop because some others can weaken the strength of the line when tied. The loop knot is well worth learning and can be used with braid, but works best with monofilament and stiff rig materials.

ANGLER FILE

Name: Bryan Jarrett
UK PB: 38lb 12oz
Age: 46
Occupation: MD, Hinders Of Swindon
Favourite water: Dinton Pastures

ANGLER FILE

Name: Mike Winstone
UK PB: 37lb 12oz
Age: 42
Occupation: Owner, bait company
Favourite water: St John's, Linear Fisheries

Day Trippers

Marc Coulson joins Bryan Jarrett and Mike Winstone as they show you how to increase your carp-catching rate on short, day sessions.

"Get on the feeder!" This common certainly liked Mike's approach.

If you thought that you have to 'camp out' for days on end to catch carp then you'd be wrong. However, if you are going to catch a few on short sessions, then you need to get your tactics right.

It was with this in mind that I asked Bryan Jarrett and Mike Winstone to show you how to do the same.

Thankfully they agreed and I find myself driving behind Bryan's car as he leads me to Tockenham Lake, near Swindon. We're soon pulling into the car park and the pair jump out of Bryan's car, ready for action. It's been an early start

and we are the first anglers on the lake.

First things first, and we set off on a stroll around the venue.

"This is the number-one rule when short-session carping – find the fish," Bryan explains.

"Although every lake has its hotspots, you should never turn up at a lake with a pre-determined idea of where you are going to fish. The carp, in any number of conditions, could be in any area of the lake."

Mike adds: "There are plenty of carp in this lake and they usually give away their location by showing themselves. If you are not watching for signs, you could easily find yourself at the wrong end of the water."

As we walk along one bank, we pass a no-fishing area, and immediately see that it is crammed full of carp. This is often the case, and carp will take refuge in such sanctuaries.

"There are so many carp in here it's untrue, and they are moving in and out of the bay, through the reeds. I think we'll start off here, Mike," Bryan says.

"When we were here earlier in the year, I caught all my fish from the entrance to the bay," Mike explained, as we walked back to the cars to get the gear.

"I did find, though, that the carp wanted the baits very tight to the reed line. I think, because it's such an obvious spot, that the fish have been pressured in this area and have become quite finicky

Bryan's Day-Session Bag Mix

1 Bryan starts off by pouring some Hinders Mini Combo pellets into a bucket.

2 He then adds the Krill 'n' Krab Multi Mix, again from Hinders.

3 Small bloodworm pellets are the next ingredient. The carp love 'em.

4 A handful of broken boilies are then added. These match his hook bait.

5 The whole lot is then mixed thoroughly until the mix is nice and even.

6 Finally, Bryan adds just enough bloodworm extract to lightly coat the mix.

The feeder rig does it again.

about picking baits up," he continued.

They soon have their kit out of the car and are ready to go.

Bryan pipes up: "Golden rule number two, mate. Don't bring the kitchen sink with you when you only have a short amount of time.

"You don't need mountains of gear and bait when only fishing for a day. It just isn't necessary. Plus, with a load of gear in your swim, you will be less inclined to move if needs be. With just a few bits and bobs, it becomes very easy to change swims if you see carp elsewhere."

Both anglers are only carrying a small amount of gear. In fact, Mike doesn't even have any alarms or banksticks with him.

"I like to just sit my rods on the floor, mate. This way I don't need to bring heavy banksticks or a pod with me.

"The only thing is, you have to sit very close to your rods, or they might get pulled in!"

As Mike lands his first carp of the day, I notice that he is using a quite different tactic from the norm. I ask him what it's all about.

"I have been playing around with these blockend feeders from Fox. I think they are great and there is a lot of mileage in their use. I fill the feeder with a mixture of crushed Mainline Pro-Active Pineapple boilies, Hinders Tiger Nut Multi Mix and some crushed hemp and this gives off a lot of attraction around the hook bait.

"The crushed boilies match my hook bait – this Pro-Active Pineapple is the dog's wotsits of a bait and I love using it. I

like to add a little of the matching Response boilie dip too, just for good measure.

"The feeder is a very easy tactic to use and requires the minimum of fuss.

I like fishing with PVA, but this has given me even more scope to experiment," Mike tells me.

Mike is indeed the type of angler who is constantly experimenting with bait and stuff, and this plays a huge part in his success. Make no mistake, he is a very talented angler and an

A chunky common falls for Bryan's bag approach.

Keep mobile, Bryan leaves most of his kit on his barrow.

absolute authority on bait. He's also a really top bloke, I might add.

After a couple of quick pictures of the carp – a small common – I nip around to the other side of the bay, where Bryan is fishing.

He only has one rod set up, although, unlike Mike, he is using banksticks and alarms.

He tells me why he only has one rod out: "I don't want to pressure the fish too much in this tight area. There are basically two spots here and Mike is fishing to one of them, so I am fishing the other. To put a second rod out would just be doing so for the sake of it, I think."

IN NO TIME AT ALL MIKE IS CALLING OVER TO ME – HE'S GOT ANOTHER ONE.

This is a valid point and, sometimes, having too many rods out can pressure the carp into clearing off. I have spoken to many fine anglers over the years who regularly use only one or two rods, regardless of how many they are allowed.

A series of bleeps emit from Bryan's alarm and he's in!

He soon has the fish – another small common – in the net and I do the honours with the camera.

"People are going to think that we have shared the same fish," Bryan jokes as he returns the carp, which is almost identical

Ready for the launch.

A bucket with a tray inside is extremely handy.

Don't take heaps of tackle on short sessions.

to the one Mike had earlier.

In no time at all Mike is calling over to me – he's got another one. I get around to his swim just as he slips it over the net.

"He's only a little 'un, shall I just slip him back without a photo?" Mike asks.

I reply that it's fine, as long as he can

Bryan's Top Bag Tips

Place the hook bait in the corner of the bag, holding the lead in your fingers.

Once the bag is filled, twist it and tie it off with some PVA tape.

A good PVA bag will be compact and have no air in it. This will cast miles.

Just to be sure it sinks immediately, pierce the bag a few times, like this.

Mike travels light, so he doesn't bother with banksticks and alarms.

Mike's Quick-Hit Feeder Tactics

1

This is one of the blockend feeders from Fox. Mike rates them highly.

2

This
He squeezes his active groundbait mix into the feeder...

3

... before replacing the end cap and casting out. Job done!

catch a few more for the cameras throughout the day.

"Yeah, definitely," comes the reply.

I joke that it's always the kiss of death when someone says that and Mike laughs in nervous agreement.

Three hours later, and with only Bryan having caught one more fish, I start to curse Mike for what he said earlier.

"I cannot believe it. I knew I shouldn't have said that," he jokes.

We have a bit of a laugh about it, but we've already done something about putting it right. We are in the third area of the lake in as many hours, moving our gear in search of carp.

Bryan's point about being able to move quickly has been proved correct, and we are basically moving around the lake and spending an hour or so in each new spot.

There are two anglers on the far bank and they have caught a couple of fish. The sun is making intermittent appearances, but when it's out it is noticeably shining on their side.

Just as one of the anglers hits a screaming run, Bryan jumps up and says: "Right, that's it. Come on Marc, we're going over there."

So it is that we are off again and we soon arrive at a swim just down the bank from where the anglers are fishing.

Bryan soon has two rods cast out, one to open water and the other down the margins to the right.

I take the opportunity to talk to him about his tactics for the day.

"I am a great believer in PVA

bags, especially on short sessions. It's no good turning up for a day's carping with loads of bait and spodding it out there, hoping that something might come along and eat it. Instead, the best tactic is to explore the water with PVA bags."

Bryan is using two tactics – one is filling a bag with crushed Pro-Active Pineapple boilies, to match his hook baits, the other is his bag mix, which you can see in Bryan's step-by-step guide.

Both are fished in solid bags, with the lead and rig inside. For this reason, Bryan points out that it's important to use very short hook links. He is using a simple rig made from Kryston Mantis and a Korda Wide Gape hook – simple rigs often work best in PVA bags.

"Once I have found some carp, I make

quite regular casts with the bag. This deposits a little bait out there, but never too much.

"It's an old saying of the match anglers, that you can put more in, but you can never take it out. This is equally as appropriate for carp anglers," he explains.

There are no carp forthcoming, so we move again.

"I cannot stress enough just how important it is to stay on the move," Mike tells me.

Before we know it, we've moved again. We've passed the car park and are just down the bank from where we started.

We've done a full circuit and, as Bryan gets another run, it has been worth it.

It's yet another small common; they're like peas in a pod in here.

"There are plenty of better fish in this lake and lots of them are mirrors. But, there are also loads of these small commons, which are normally quite obliging when the big 'uns don't play ball," Mike tells me, as he lands another of the little bars of gold.

One more fish is caught at the new spot, before it goes quiet again. We make one last move back to the bay and the duo help themselves to another common each.

It's soon time to leave. It's been a great day's fishing and I thank them both for their time, efforts and great company.

Kept it simple on short sessions and you'll catch.

The rig that did the business for Mike.

Mike and Bryan have worked hard to find and catch the carp – a great lesson to all of you out there that fish short sessions. Give Mike and Bryan's tactics a try – stay mobile and catch some carp.

Mastermind

Dave Lane, one of the country's best carp anglers, answers questions on all things carpy.

Q For more sensitive bite indication, do you always recommend using slack lines?

A Without going into a great big epic on this subject, which I often do when prompted, I'll try and relate my findings, gathered through trial and experimentation over the years.

Firstly, to fish a tight line, you need to introduce a certain amount of stretch into the line. As you tighten down to the lead, the line will stretch considerably before the bobbin sits tightly under the rod.

Now that everything is set you are using semi-stretched line, with no further vertical movement available on the bobbin. Therefore, a fish will need to remove all the remaining stretch, which is considerable, before exerting enough pressure to engage the Baitrunner, clutch or free-spool facility.

Likewise, with drop-back movement the fish has to move towards you, far enough to release the stretch you have created, before the bobbin can drop.

With a slack line, every single movement is instantly transmitted through the line. Trust me, you would find the results amazing and unbelievable.

Obviously, there are many situations, such as flowing or drifting water, big winds and so on, where a slack line is not feasible or practicable, but there is still no need to introduce stretch. I simply set up slack and slowly tighten until the bobbin can just about hold its own weight. This gives me the best of both worlds.

A fish does not have to remove any stretch before registering a bite because the weight of the bobbin is less than the force needed to stretch monofilament. As a result, any movement is

instantly transmitted to the rod and alarm.

An easy and revealing test is to set up as normal but point the rod along the bank (or a big field). Walk the rig along the bank, at least 50 or 60 yards, or even further, and set it on the floor before returning to the rod and setting up a tight line.

Using a sounder box, or a loud alarm, you can try moving the rig forwards and backwards as I have done here in the pictures.

You can see from the stick markers that I managed a full three feet before I had a single indication on the alarm. Even then it was only one bleep, and the next bleep seemed to bear no relation to anything I did at my end.

Drop backs were also just as unresponsive, but the worst by far was side-to-side movement. I just didn't have enough bank space to make the alarm sound even a single bleep!

If you imagine a situation where

you are fishing up against a snaggy island margin, where the only movement a fish can make is towards you, or, more likely, a sideways movement, then you can see the problems this will create.

I am not advocating fishing a totally slack line against snags but, as I have outlined above, if you remove all the stretch from the line first, your indication will definitely be improved.

If you now try the same exercise with a totally slack line that lays flat to the ground, you will see a different result altogether.

On this test, I didn't even manage to lift the lead off the ground before the first bleep sounded and the alarm was going mad as I slowly increased the distance from the stick. Drop backs and side movement were also far more responsive and there really was a world of difference between the two methods.

Indication on a tight line is poor. The rig could be moved this far before the alarm sounded.

On a slack line the rig only moved a few inches before the alarm sounded.

On a tight line a fish could kite this far to the right or left before registering a bite.

Dawn 'Til Dusk

Colin Davidson doesn't bother with bivvies and bedchairs in winter. He makes the most of day sessions and the first few hours of darkness. Here's how...

It's rare you'll find me carrying bedchairs, five-season sleeping bags, thermal covers, bivvies or winter skins at this time of year. Much of my winter fishing revolves around day sessions, or even shorter afternoon and evening trips. The simplicity of a day session appeals much more than camping through 14 hours of darkness. Why not lose the bivvy and try day trips instead?

It amazes me that some anglers don't feel it's worth going fishing unless

ANGLER FILE

Name: Colin Davidson
Age: 30
UK PB: 43lb 3oz
Hometown: Grays, Essex
Favourite water: Arena, Essex

Dawn and dusk can be productive times in winter.

Keep feed to a minimum on short sessions, so try using stringers.

You'll be needing these if you're fishing into darkness.

they've got at least 24 hours. I've always fished short trips quite happily, and winter is one of the best times to cut rod hours down and make your time on the bank more productive.

Short trips are most effective when you're fishing close to home and visiting a water regularly, even if that's only once a week. The name of the game is getting a few bites as regularly as possible, with the chance of a decent fish thrown in. It has been said many times, but make sure you pick a water with a good head of carp, perhaps a well-stocked day ticket water. These venues produce action more reliably when the weather has turned for the worse.

GET THE FEEDING SPELLS RIGHT AND YOU CAN FISH FEWER HOURS AT THE BEST TIMES.

So, if you've got a productive venue nearby and you fancy some short-session action in winter, how do you go about it?

The single biggest reason why short trips can be so successful at this time of year is the pronounced tendency for carp to feed for short spells at particular times. Feeding behaviour can, and does, become very fixed, meaning that if you can find the times when carp are being

caught, you can fish fewer hours but at the best times.

Some waters I've fished have been best for a bite mid-morning, whereas others tend to be mid-afternoon. The only way you'll find the pattern to any feeding spells is by being there. So for your first few trips to a new, or even familiar venue, it's advisable to fish the whole day. This will help to get a picture of when the carp are most active, or when you see fish caught or catch them yourself. A mate of mine spent much of last winter fishing 'office hours' and caught stacks. He tried earlier and later but the best times, conveniently, were during office hours, so that's when he fished.

Bailiffs and other anglers can also be

very helpful, so make a note what time other carp are caught, or ask what time of day people have had their action. It's not like you're asking them what bait they're using, where they're casting or what rigs they're using, so normally it's easy enough to get a straight answer.

For this feature we visited Bayeswater day ticket lake and it was extremely quiet all morning. The only indicator action I had was a short pull as soon as I cast out when I arrived. Talking to Steve, the

Winter-Session Tips

1
Try a pellet-shaped boilie instead of a round-shaped one. It may get you extra bites.

2
Paste oozes attraction. Try wrapping your boilie in a matching paste.

3
Have plenty of rigs tied up before you start. On day trips, time is limited.

bailiff, later that day, he told me that he'd had three takes the day before, all between 8am and 8.30am – which was when I'd arrived – and nothing for the rest of the day. Oops, I should have got out of bed earlier! If I was going back to Bayeswater the following week it would have made sense to get there a couple of hours earlier, to see if there was still a pronounced feeding spell early morning. Short trips or day sessions can be great, but you can also miss a lot of action if you don't keep an eye and an ear on what is happening on your venue.

The shorter the trip, the more important it is to increase your chances of having a hook bait picked up quickly. This means that whenever I'm day fishing it's rare for me to introduce free offerings.

I WANT A BITE STRAIGHTAWAY – THAT MEANS SINGLE HOOK BAITS.

I don't have days on end and hundreds of kilos of boilies to prebait swims. I want to get a bite straightaway, and that means single hook baits, bags or stringers. I don't see any point in introducing bait when I'm fishing during the day, especially on waters I don't know very well, because it's either eaten by seagulls or

picked up off the bottom by coots and tufties. One bait, or a little mouthful in the right place, is more than enough to catch a carp, even on the hardest of waters. Besides, if you're moving hook baits about regularly to try and find some carp and get a bite, the last thing you want is a pouchful of boilies in every spot you've tried.

If you're returning to a venue, it can help to drop a bit of bait in when you leave. By this time you will hopefully have a better idea of where the carp are and be able to put the bait in front of them instead of guessing. Plus, by putting it in after dark you give the carp an extra 10 or 12 hours to find it before the birds. Don't go mad either, just a couple of hundred baits in a few likely areas is more than enough to give them a taste.

The biggest mistake when day fishing in winter is to pack up too early. If your venue allows it, your chances of action get better and better if you can stay after dark. One of the patterns I've seen on most lakes I've winter fished is that most carp activity is late in the day, or into the first couple of hours of darkness.

With the numbers of cormorants around these days, nocturnal carp activity is more pronounced. In big winds or mild

weather you might see carp jumping and getting caught all day, but it's more often the case that they seem only to stir late afternoon as the sun drops.

On a venue I've never seen or fished before I might be there from first thing, but if I had to put money on getting action it would be mid to late afternoon onwards. These are the golden hours and the first couple into darkness can see a lake come to life after being dead all day. Wherever possible, stay for a couple of hours after dark.

Just because it's dark doesn't mean you suddenly need a bivvy or a sleeping bag. It's only 5pm and if you've been warm enough all day under a brolly, your thermals aren't suddenly going to let you down because the lights have gone off. As long as you've got a headtorch and a spare, you can fish on quite happily.

Location is everything in winter and it

Winter feeding times can be very localised, so make a note of them.

Colin uses insulating tape to mark his lines.

Try These Tips For More Bites

A small stringer of halved boilies has accounted for loads of winter carp.

Try using small PVA bags filled with liquidised bread — it really works.

Running rigs are excellent at registering shy bites from wary carp.

Baiting up in the dark is a great tactic, but one that's rarely used.

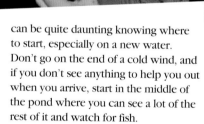

can be quite daunting knowing where to start, especially on a new water. Don't go on the end of a cold wind, and if you don't see anything to help you out when you arrive, start in the middle of the pond where you can see a lot of the rest of it and watch for fish.

Carp showing is the best sign of all that you're in front of fish and in the right place. However, in poor conditions, even if you're watching hard, you might see nothing for most of the day. Keep an eye on other anglers to see if anyone else is catching and, most importantly, use your lines as a location tool.

They are the best insight you've got into what is going on under the water. I use light bobbins and slack lines, with banksticks pointing at my baits wherever possible, so if there are any numbers of carp in front of me I'll get line bites. More often than not the prime time for getting a line bite is just after casting, when your line is settling down through the water. I slacken line off the rod tip after I've put the rod on the rests and keep an eye on the line of the rod tip for a couple of minutes. Sometimes you just see it rise and fall or flick up and down quickly a few times, as it is brushed by a fish or

A cracking winter twenty, taken on a paste-wrapped bottom bait.

picked up by a fin. Even if you're not seeing carp or catching them, casting in different spots in front of you throughout the day can give you some useful information as to where your best chance of a bite may be and where to concentrate your efforts and other rods.

Remember though, that it may be right towards the end of the day that you see any signs of carp showing, and this is the time to get hook baits on them or even move swim if you're in totally the wrong place. I've lost count of the number of winter carp I've caught after casting at showing fish late in the day, or within minutes of moving swims to get on them.

Try and have stringers and bags ready and your gear tidied away, so whatever you see towards dusk you can react to. Often, you can wind a rod in and get a bait on a showing carp while the disturbance it's made is still visible.

Expect and be prepared for that spell of activity late in the day and be able to take advantage. Don't ignore one or two carp showing, they might be the only ones you see and they could give away the location of an entire shoal. Even if they don't, you can bet they won't be on their own and a bait in the right place, even just for an hour or two, is worth many hours camped in the wrong place.

Rig Zone

Which three rigs does Mike Winstone put all his faith in, and how do you tie them? Read on and find out...

Have you ever wondered whether the 'name' anglers use the same rigs as you? Or do they use secret rigs that you've never heard of, and which do they have absolute confidence in? We set out to answer these questions.

If you're at a bit of a loss when it comes to tying an ultra-effective rig, or just want something new to try, then check this out. You never know, one of Mike Winstone's three all-time favourite rigs may give you the edge you've been looking for.

"There are so many factors that lead to catching a carp," says Mike. "Rigs are just a small, but vital, ingredient. Unfortunately, there is no such thing as a wonder rig. A lot of people are under the false impression that most of the 'named' anglers have secret, wonder rigs, which is why they catch so many fish. Wrong. Almost all of the successful anglers I know stick to two or three rigs that they have complete faith in. Their success comes from their vast experience, knowledge of carp behaviour and outstanding watercraft. That said, if your rig doesn't work then everything else is pointless.

ANGLER FILE

Name: Mike Winstone
Nickname: Iron Mike
Age: 42
Location: Dursley
UK PB: 37lb 12oz

"Before I get into the mechanics of my three rigs, and when to use each one, I'm going to highlight a few points that you might pick up on throughout this piece.

"The barbed-versus-barbless hook debate has been going for years and will continue for many years to come. I doubt there will ever be a definite answer, but I always use barbless hooks. Years ago, when I started carp fishing, barbed hooks were more 'savage' than they are nowadays and a carp's mouth could be easily damaged during the unhooking process. For this reason I opted to use barbless hooks and have had no reason to change. I don't have to change my rigs depending on the fishery rules either, because 99 per cent of fisheries allow barbless hooks. I would like to point out that I don't think there's a problem with the modern barbed hooks, but problems can arise during the unhooking process if the angler is relatively inexperienced.

USING BENT SHRINK TUBING IS VITAL TO MY RIGS' MECHANICS.

"All three of the rigs I've outlined in this feature use baits mounted on a rig ring. Not only does the ring allow the hook bait a great deal of movement but it makes the rig more versatile than a standard hair rig. As the hook bait is tied to the ring and there is no set 'hair length' I can change the size and shape of the hook bait without having to tie a new rig.

"No doubt you will notice that all three of these rigs have a right-angled bend just above the eye of the hook. This is created using either shrink tubing or a stiff hooklength material, depending on the rig. This bend is vital to the mechanics of the rig. It helps the hook flip and 'grab hold' in the carp's mouth and makes the hook much harder for the fish to eject. Think about it, a 'bent' hooklength is much harder to spit out than a straight one.

"Right then, onto the rigs. I refer to my first rig as a PVA-bag rig simply because it's the rig I use inside solid PVA bags. However, it's more of a general-purpose rig and can be used for anything from single-hook-bait fishing through to the Method feeder. It can be used with bottom baits and pop-ups too. This rig is so

Mike's PVA-Bag Rig

1. You will need a coated hooklength material, a rig ring, shrink tubing and a hook.

2. Strip back six to eight inches of the plastic coating from the hooklength material.

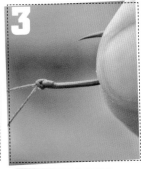

3. Tie your chosen hook to the exposed braid using a palomar knot.

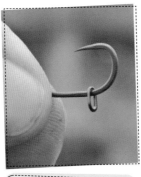

Place a small rig ring onto the shank of the hook. Oval and round rings both work.

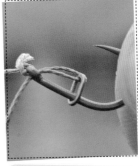

Pass a length of braid through the eye, then the ring and back through the eye.

Tie a simple overhand knot in the braid behind the eye of the hook.

Push a 1in length of shrink tubing over the eye. Note the ring's position.

Using steam from a kettle shrink the tubing at a right angle to the hook shank.

The finished rig. Note the stripped coating directly behind the tubing.

versatile that if I were restricted to using one rig for all of my angling, this would be it. Although I tie this rig using a coated braid, Armaled's Kik-Bak to be precise, it can be tied with all manner of materials and works just as well if tied with mono or braid. If you do use a coated braid then strip about 2mm of coating from directly behind the shrink

Mike's Pop-Up Rig

1 Place a Wychwood crimp followed by a swivel onto a length of Amnesia.

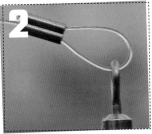

2 Pass the Amnesia through the crimp, blob the end with a lighter and pull it tight to the crimp.

3 Flatten the crimp with a Wychwood Crimp Tool. It's easy to do and won't slip.

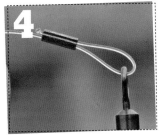

4 The swivel should now be on a small loop. This aids movement of the hooklength.

5 Attach a Solar Micro Swivel tight to the crimp on the other end of the Amnesia.

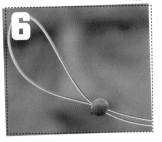

6 Take a length of 22lb Subterfuge, loop it over and thread on a small, hard bead.

7 Tie an overhand knot in the Subterfuge and blob the tag ends.

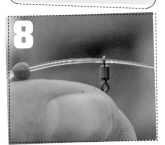

8 Pass the Subterfuge loop through the Solar Micro Swivel; it will be a tight fit.

9 Now pass the loop through the eye of your chosen hook. Mike uses a Korda Wide Gape B.

10 Pass the end of the loop over the point of the hook and pull it tight.

11 Thread a small rig ring, followed by a Fox Ring Stop, onto the shank of the hook.

12 Here's the finished rig. Note the curve of the hook section and the position of the hook.

tubing. This adds extra movement to the hook and hook bait and definitely makes the rig work better than if all the coating was left on.

"My next offering is my pop-up rig. I came up with this a while ago and have yet to find a more effective way of presenting a pop-up. It incorporates a short hook section, the length of which determines how high off the lake bed the bait sits, and a stiff, boom section. You might notice, if you look at the pictures, that the hook section is curved slightly. This helps the hook flip around and 'grab hold' in the carp's mouth as soon as the bait is inhaled. A Fox Ring Stop is placed on the hook opposite the hook point that, once the rig is baited and in the water, makes the hook sit parallel to the lake bed. When a fish closes its mouth around the

bait the hook point comes into contact with the carp's mouth almost instantly. Any stiff material will suffice for making the boom section, but I prefer to use Amnesia. A few months ago I started using the Wychwood crimps for making the boom sections and I have to say, they're awesome. I've always found tying loops and knots in stiff materials extremely difficult and these crimps eliminate all of the problems. They're strong, neat, easy to use and I would recommend them to anyone using stiff materials.

"Using crimps for making the boom section, together with the swivel and weight of the hook, means that, providing you use a pop-up of 14mm or smaller, you don't need to add any extra weight to sink the hook bait. If you use a bigger pop-up and do require extra weight then place a shot or lump of putty on the upright, hook section of the rig, not on the stiff boom. Remember to test the rig in the margins to ensure it sits properly before you cast out. You don't want to be fishing this rig with a bait that sinks or one that's too buoyant.

"When fishing over a bed of boilies and the fish are picking up individual baits, rather than hoovering the lake bed, the pop-up rig is my choice. In this instance I make the hook section as short as I can, to get the bait close to the lake bed.

"Believe it or not, this rig can be used inside a PVA bag too. The hook section of the rig can be placed inside a small PVA bag along with some pellets or bag mix. But do not try and cram the stiff boom section into the bag as well; it won't work.

"If the carp become quite finicky or I want to use a straight bottom bait then the bottom-bait rig is by far the best choice. This is the most straightforward of the three rigs to tie and incorporates a fluorocarbon hooklength, knotless knot and a small rig ring. If you look at the step-by-step you will notice that the ring is tied tight to the hook. This is simply because I like to get the bait as close to the hook as I can.

"All of my rigs are tied from stiff, or semi-stiff materials. I think these sit on the lake bed much better than supple, braided hooklengths and don't tangle or coil up on the cast. Like most things in this sport, the hooklength material is very much a personal thing. What works for one angler won't necessarily work for the next. The best advice I can give you is to experiment.

"You learn a lot about the way rigs work by experimenting with different rigs in different situations. A simple way of determining whether your rig is working

Mike's Bottom-Bait Rig

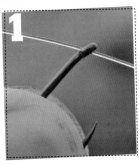

Thread your chosen hook onto a length of stiff material. Mike favours Amnesia.

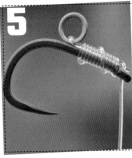

Next, thread a small rig ring onto the hooklength. Round and oval rings both work well.

Hold the ring opposite the hook point and the tag end against the shank of the hook.

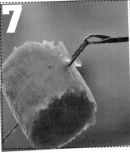

Whip the hooklength back up the hook, trapping the tag end in place.

Pull the ring tight to the shank of the hook and trim off the tag end.

Tie a small loop in a length of thin braid. Mike uses Kryston Samson hair braid.

Using a baiting needle, thread your chosen hook bait onto the thin braid.

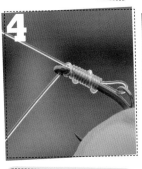

Pass the end of the braid through the ring, tight to the shank of the hook.

Pull the bait tight to the ring and tie it in place using a couple of overhand knots.

properly, and how the fish are feeding, is to check the position of the hook in the carp's mouth. If they're not really 'having it' the fish will probably be lightly hooked in the lips. With a few simple alterations to your rig you can put a lot more fish on the bank. Again it's a case of trial and error.

"One problem that can be remedied quite quickly is hook-pulls. Changing the size of your hook is an effective way to reduce them. A bigger hook isn't always the answer.

Sometimes a smaller hook will put more carp on the bank.

"Checking your rigs is of utmost importance. Before every cast check that your hook points are sharp, all the knots are in perfect condition and the hook itself isn't damaged. It's no good using the best rig in the world if the hook point is damaged, or it breaks as soon as you hook a fish.

"As I said, there are no wonder rigs. If you do happen to come across one then please let me know! In all seriousness, the best advice I can give you is to find a rig that works for you and stick with it."

Alright on The Night

Get the most from your first night session with these 10 top tips...

In the springtime many carp anglers dust off their bivvies and start thinking about fishing a few night sessions. Many of you may also be thinking about fishing an overnighter for the very first time. But what do you need and, once there, how do you maximise your chances of catching after dark?

We met up with carp expert and regular overnighter Tony Makepeace, with a brief to look at how to go about your night fishing.

Tony fishes lots of night sessions and has had considerable success, so we asked him to pass on what he thinks are some of the most important things to get right, including what you need to take with you to make your overnight stay as enjoyable and productive as possible.

ANGLER FILE

Name: Tony Makepeace
Age: 33
Occupation: Carp consultant, Banks & Burr
UK PB: 36lb 11oz
Nicknames: Dempsey, Codpiece

Tip One
Cover Up

A good bivvy is essential and will help you stay comfortable at night. Even in the summer this country's weather can be unpredictable, and you don't want to get caught out.

Imagine fishing your first night session and having a brolly uprooted by strong winds, or a sudden rainstorm soaking you to the skin. Your first session will soon turn into a nightmare and you won't want to go again!

If you are even remotely thinking about possible winter or even autumn night trips, you'll also want an extra skin for your bivvy. I use a Chub bivvy and also have the extended second skin because, as well as the insulation that it offers, the porch area gives me some storage space for muddy boots and the like.

Try and get yourself the best shelter you can afford – it'll be one of the best investments

Tip Two
Get Into The Comfort Zone

Many of the early pioneers of carp fishing talk of the good old days when they would grab a few hours' shuteye on a deck chair or similar, but these days there are several ways of ensuring that you are much more comfortable.

I have recently worn out my old Sundridge sleeping bag that I have had for years. It was a great bag, but finally fell to bits through overuse.

I've since got myself a brand new bag from Trakker and it is brilliant. Being able to sleep in comfort and warmth is essential for the night angler.

A decent bedchair also helps with this. Now, this might sound strange, but you should also try and get your bedchair as level as possible – this really does make a difference to how soundly you sleep.

Tip **Three**
Munch Up

At any time of the year, it is essential to keep fed and watered. I take all the essentials, such as kettle, stoves, tea, coffee, milk and sugar, but also make sure I have plenty of food with me. Well, actually, my missus takes the trouble to make sure I have food – thanks Sharon!

In the winter I always take something that I can heat up in a pan, rather than just sandwiches. It's vital to keep drinking all year round and, in the winter especially, it's important to eat some hot food.

I take a gas stove in the summer and always make sure I have enough spare gas with me. However, in the winter, gas stoves can be prone to not working, so in the colder months I always take a petrol-fuelled stove as well, just in case. My Coleman will work whatever the temperature. It's better to be safe than sorry.

Tip **Four**
Sort It!

Some of my mates take the mick out of me as my bivvy is always immaculate inside. What I mean by this is that everything is in its place and all the essentials are tidy and to hand.

If I wake up in the night to the sound of a run, the last thing I need is to be fumbling around in my bivvy looking for my headtorch or my boots.

Equally, with all my tackle neat and tidy, I know where everything is if I need to re-tie a rig with only my headtorch for light.

I always make sure that my landing net is near my rods and that I have the unhooking mat and sling in the right place, before I go to bed for the night.

Tip **Five**
Wrap Up!

Believe it or not, the tin in the picture is actually the packaging for some new thermal underclothing from Greys, who I am a consultant for.

It's important that, as well as being warm in your sleeping bag, you should do all you can to remain warm at night when out of your bag.

It's no good being all snug in your bag and then dashing out to hit a run in just your pants! Well, not in the winter anyway.

In the summer, a light layer of clothing is more appropriate and will also help guard against mozzie bites in the evening and early morning.

I always have a spare set of clothing, just in case I have to get out of my bag in the night and it's raining. I do not want to have to get back into my sleeping bag soaking wet.

Tip Six
Shine A Light

This might sound a bit of an obvious one, but I have seen many anglers overlook one of the most important items of tackle... a headtorch. I carry two, in case one should ever pack up, and take loads of spare batteries for each.

I also have a light in my bivvy, for those occasions when I need to clip a bag on or get some gear out of my bag. I've been playing around with a night-light from Chub, which is sound activated. By leaving it next to my alarm remote, I have instant lighting every time I get a run! Don't overdo it with the lights though, or you might incur the wrath of other anglers on the water. Besides, if your bivvy is lit up like Blackpool promenade, the fish won't come anywhere near you. Don't say I didn't warn you!

Tip Seven
Isotopia

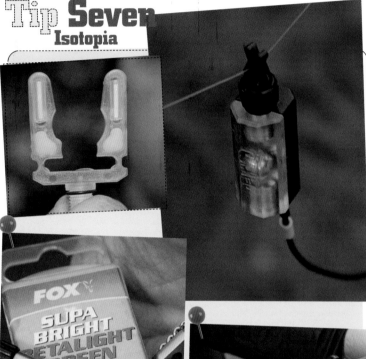

As well as headtorches and the like, a bit of illumination on your bite indicators helps no end.

I use Delkim alarms along with the matching hangers. These feature a small light in the head that lights up at the same time that the alarm head does.

I am not suggesting you all go out and buy Delkims, but what I would say, though, is to use hangers that have slots for isotopes. This means that you can see any movements on your hanger in the dark. I have recently got myself a set of backrests from Enterprise, which boasts small isotopes inside.

I also use some small isotopes in my landing-net arms. These help massively when I'm trying to get a carp into the net in the middle of the night.

Tip Eight
Come On Arsenal!

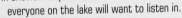

While I do not like anglers who take televisions onto the bank with them – it can be noisy and stop you from concentrating on your angling – I do always take my radio.

Night fishing on your own, especially in the winter, when the nights are very long, can be a solitary affair and the radio is a welcome companion. I listen to all sorts of programmes, from football commentaries and music to those hilarious late-night phone-in shows. Keep the volume down though, as not everyone on the lake will want to listen in.

Tip Nine
Glow-In-The-Dark Baits

Yes, they really do exist. Many of you will have seen the new glow-in-the-dark stuff from the likes of Enterprise and Alien Baits. The jury is still out on these for me, but I am playing around with a few.

I also use quite a lot of high-attract baits at night, particularly the ones that smell a lot. I was never sure how well carp could see at night and thought they would probably rely on smell to find food. Then, a while ago, I fished with Marc Coulson down Oxford way and he caught a couple in the night on single grains of plastic corn. That got me thinking about the visual aspect.

I use Premier Baits for all my fishing and have no reason to stop using it at night. I've caught loads on it in both the day and night and have the utmost confidence in it during darkness. Most baits that work in the day will do so at night, but don't be afraid to experiment with some of the luminous stuff.

Tip Ten
On The Mark

Part of the daytime preparation theme is to find your fishing spots in daylight, with the use of a marker float. It is very difficult to do this at night.

Once you have located a decent spot, pop your float up and cast your rig to it. Try and find a far-bank marker at this point, a tree or something similar that you can see at night. Once you are happy that the rig has landed on the spot, mark the line just above the reel with a marker-braid or pole-elastic knot.

This way, if you need to recast at night, you simply cast the rig down the lake and wind back until the marker is in place. Next, put your line in the clip on your reel and wind in. Now, cast towards the far-bank marker and let the line-clip do the rest. With practice you learn to gauge when the line will hit the clip, and then cushion the impact with the rod.

To make baiting up easier at night, I have attached a couple of Drennan Starlights to my marker float. This makes the float visible at night, so I can catapult my boilies around it.

Mastermind

Dave Lane, one of the country's best carp anglers, answers questions on all things carpy.

Q How do you prepare for a safe night session?

A To fish safely at night you first have to sort out, during the daylight, everything that you might need after dark. This way you will be able to go straight to any item without searching around in the dark, especially if you have a fish on the bank.

Your torch is obviously a very important item and needs to always be to hand. I always hang mine on the adjuster wheel of my bedchair; this way I always know where it is. A good plan is to have a spare torch in a side pocket of the rucksack, where it can be easily found if the first one fails.

I tend to keep every item of tackle I possess in the same place at all times; I reckon that I can find anything I need in the pitch black, even without a torch, or at least that's the theory.

Any items that you need in order to deal with a fish can be left outside the bivvy already laid out or, if there is a security problem with leaving your gear outside, just keep it all on the unhooking mat, just inside your door. Things you will need to hand include an unhooking mat, forceps, water, weigh sling, scales and a carp sack (if they are allowed).

Obviously, from a comfort point of view, you should arrange your gear in a manner that will make fishing in the dark comfortable and safe. Don't have any eye-level branches or things you can trip over between your bed and the rods. Make sure your boots are easily accessible and have your landing net set out in a sensible spot. Plan the fight with a fish in advance to allow for weed beds, snags and suchlike,

Make sure there are no obstacles between your bed and your rods.

so you know exactly what to do. It's also worth noting any far-bank markers on the skyline, like trees and buildings, so that you can recast in the dark if you need to. Make sure the markers are on the skyline though as, once dark, you will not see anything that has a load of trees behind it, like a far-bank bush or reeds

for example. Similarly, don't pick a far-bank marker that's likely to move, such as a cow.

Ideally, you want to be fishing a safe and secure venue that you are familiar with. It would also be handy to have the bailiff's number on your mobile just in case you experience any problems, of whatever kind.

Place your headtorch over the handwheel on your bedchair.

Essential items should be kept under the head of the bedchair.

Forceps are attached to the side of the shelter so they don't get lost.

All you need is Vision...

Method mixes • Pellets
Shelf life birdfood and fishmeal
boilies • Freezer baits
Hydro Shelf life boilies
Base mixes • Bulk food oils
Pop-ups • Hookbait enhancers
Liquid foods • Pellet booster oils
• Natural extracts • Nature
identical concentrates

AVAILABLE AT ALL GOOD TACKLE SHOPS

FREE Catalogue on request

Visionbaits International

Mile End Business Park, Oswestry, Shropshire SY10 8NN
Telephone: +44 (0)1691 659859 • Fax: +44 (0)1691 671487

Email: sales@visionbaitsint.com
A member of the Morgans Group

PVA

Get the basics right and you'll be well on the way to catching more carp...

Month after month you read about anglers catching carp on PVA bags, but how do you tie them and what should you put in them? There are loads of PVA products out there, so which should you be using?

PVA bags are a very effective way of catching carp, especially on short day sessions, so learning how to tie one properly is well worth it. Be it a big solid bag filled with some sort of 'bag mix' or a tiny stocking-type bag holding just a pinch of pellets, don't be afraid to cast a PVA bag out nearly every time.

There is no definitive answer to which type is best because each has its uses. The thing to do is get yourself some PVA bags and stocking and experiment. There is no end to what you can put in them, so you can deposit a nice tidy pile of whatever you want around your hook bait. Many anglers even cast out a PVA bag with just a liquid attractor inside it. Beware though, don't use a water-based liquid or the bag will melt!

Here, we've shown you a couple of ways that you can use PVA – a solid bag and a stocking bag. The stocking is the simplest and most user-friendly, but don't be afraid to have a go with the solid bags too. With a little practice you will master them and they could just help you catch your next carp.

Stocking PVA Bags – The Easy Way

It's always a good idea to mix up the sizes of pellets you put into PVA...

... so we've added 4mm and 3mm versions. These are halibut pellets.

In order that your hook bait matches the bait in the bag, add a crushed boilie or two.

Add your mixed pellets to the PVA, which already contains your crushed boilies.

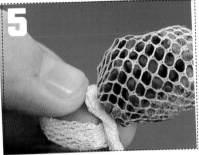

Compact the contents in the PVA and tie off the bag as tightly as possible, like this.

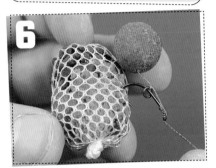

Nick your baited hook into the PVA bag and you're ready to go. This catches loads of carp.

Solid PVA Bags – Give Them A Go

Place your baited hook into the corner of your PVA bag and add a little of your mix.

You can now add more mix over the top of the rig. Using a spoon makes this far easier.

Once the bag is half full, add your lead. The mix in the bag will support this.

Fill the bag to about two-thirds full and twist the excess PVA, like this.

Use PVA tape to tie off the bag. Keep the bag as tight as possible when doing this.

Trim the excess PVA and then carefully pierce the bag with a needle.

You too can catch carp like this 34lb stunner. Just follow Ian's advice.

Big-Carp Tactics

Where do you go and what tactics do you use to catch carp as big as this one? Ian Russell reveals all.

When somebody starts carp fishing the first thing they want to do is bag a big carp. While the ultimate goal in our sport is to catch big fish, I can't stress how important it is to work your way up from the bottom; serve your 'apprenticeship' as it were.

ANGLER FILE

Name: Ian 'Chemo' Russell
Age: 44
Occupation: Partner, Heathrow Bait Services
Favourite water: Savay
UK PB: 43lb 9oz

Start off by catching singles and doubles and aim to slowly up the size of the carp you're catching. Jumping in at the deep end and targeting a massive fish from the word go will not only prove very difficult and frustrating for you, but, should you catch your target fish, you could also put its life at risk if you don't have the experience of dealing with carp of that size.

Before I get into how to catch big carp, let's get the safety aspect out of the way. I've already mentioned that you need to know how to handle big carp, but having the right gear when you do catch that fish of a lifetime is equally as important. A decent unhooking mat, quality weigh sling, big landing net and a good set of scales are must-have items, as is a decent camera. After all, you'll want to document the occasion.

Big day ticket carp aren't as difficult to catch as a lot of anglers will have you

believe. A big carp is basically an eating machine and needs to consume a lot of food. All you need to do is get your bait in the right place at the right time and the rest should fall into place. Well, in a perfect world it would be that simple, but as I'm constantly reminded we don't live in a perfect world.

There are a few steps that you can take to maximise your chances of banking that fish of a lifetime. The preparation for your session should start at home. First of all, you need to decide on a venue to target. By picking a venue with a good head of big carp, rather than one with thousands of doubles and a thirty, you've increased your chances before you've even left the house. I enjoy my fishing and don't want to sit on the bank worrying about how safe my car is or whether my gear is going to be nicked. Therefore it pays to pick a secure venue with a good track record, such as Farlows

The Wriggler Rig

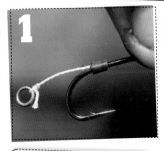

1

Tie up a standard rig using a knotless knot and attach a ring to the end of the hair.

2

Thread a length of dental floss or thin braid through the eye of a needle.

3

Carefully, thread 15 to 20 maggots onto the needle, taking care not to burst them.

4

Push the maggots and a bit of rig foam onto the dental floss and tie it in an overhand knot.

5

Pass one end of the dental floss through the ring on the hair and tie two overhand knots.

6

Using a pair of scissors or a sharp knife, trim off the tag ends of the dental floss.

7

Test the rig in the edge. Trim pieces off the rig foam until the hook just sinks.

8

Attach a PVA bag of maggots onto the rig. Use two pieces of PVA foam to cover the hook.

Make sure your gear's up to the job. Big carp fight hard.

Conceal your rig if fishing on gravel.

Lake, any of the Linear Fisheries waters or CEMEX Sandhurst Lake to name a few. By keeping an eye on the angling press and looking at the catch reports you can see which venues are producing and, usually, what baits are working too.

By remaining in touch with the carp scene via websites, talking to other anglers, tackle-shop owners and the like, you can often find out when a venue is producing in time to get in on the action. If you target a specific venue for any length of time it's always worth spending a day or two 'walking and talking'. Walk the banks of your chosen venue and chat to the other anglers; you'll be amazed at what you learn.

Once you've chosen a venue to target, you can then narrow down exactly when your best chances will be. Personally, I target big carp in autumn and spring. The reason for this is simple; it's when they really get their heads down and feed hard, either because they're feeding up for the winter or have just come out of 'hibernation'. At these times of year the big carp seem to drop their guard slightly as they go about eating as much as possible, which in turn makes them more catchable. If you get to know a venue and its inhabitants you'll find that the bigger fish inhabit certain areas of a lake at certain times of the year. By concentrating on these areas and spending as much time as

you can in them, you should cross paths with your quarry eventually. Big carp are generally creatures of habit and will follow the same routine year after year, so once you've sussed their movements you can return time and time again. As well as the time of year, the weather conditions have a huge impact on the carp's behaviour. As a general rule, low-pressure weather systems always produce big carp and if you can get out on the banks during a spell of stormy weather then you're in a good position. Over the years I've found that weather

If you're catching tench then your rigs are working fine.

Big commons are more wary than big mirrors.

systems with a westerly wind produce carp, so that's one to look out for. On the other hand, bright and clear conditions make for generally very poor fishing times, especially in the winter.

As I said before, big carp will inhabit certain areas of a lake but, once you've located the right area, you still need to find a spot to place your hook bait. It's common practice to turn up in a swim, chuck out a marker rod and cast to the first bit of gravel you find. But remember, if you can find that feature then everybody else that fishes that swim can find it too. That's not to say the feature won't produce, but try and do something a little different to everybody else. I've taken more big carp off the front of gravel bars, fishing on the edge of the silt, than I have fishing on top of them. I'm sure it's because most people fish right on top of the bars, so the carp get wary of feeding on them. A bait sitting in the silt next to the bar is a much safer option as far as they're concerned.

I'm often asked if big carp are smarter than small carp and therefore harder to catch? As a general rule, I would have to say: "No." All pressured

carp learn how to 'deal' with rigs and even the small carp can get rid of a rig with surprising ease once they've been hooked a couple of times. A carp doesn't suddenly get smarter once it breaks the 20lb barrier! Big carp just get caught less than small

ANGLERS BELIEVE A FISH WON'T GET CAUGHT AGAIN FOR A WHILE. RUBBISH!

carp, because there are less of them! However, I would say that big commons are more wary than big mirrors. Big carp are extremely greedy fish and on numerous occasions I've witnessed big mirrors muscle other fish off a baited spot and then rip the bottom up, eating every

morsel of food they find. Big commons, on the other hand, tend to hang back off the bait and observe what's going on before slowly moving in to feed.

Another common misconception about big carp is that if a target fish has been caught anglers believe it won't get caught again for a while. Some anglers even go as far as moving to another venue for a few weeks. Rubbish! The fact is that these carp are very big fish and start feeding again quite quickly after being returned. And if they're feeding you can catch them. I can recall two occasions when I've been fishing with my mate Garth and he's caught a 40lb-plus carp, then I've caught the same fish just four days later. One was the awesome Shoulders from Horton and the other was a 43lb fully scaled from a

Using The Stick

Using some slightly damp groundbait and narrow PVA, make a small bait stick.

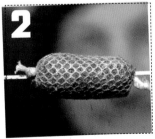

Pass a stringer needle through the centre of the stick, as shown here.

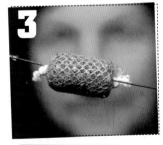

Attach your rig to the needle and pull it back through the centre of the stick.

Pull the stick down your hooklength until your hook sits inside the base of it.

Big carp will inhabit certain areas of a lake. Find them and you're in the box seats.

private syndicate lake.

A stumbling block for many anglers when they get to a lake is how much bait to introduce? Should you put more bait in if you're after big carp? Do you pile it all in at the start or wait until you've had a bite? Do you use single hook baits, bags or a big bed of pellets and should you continue to feed throughout the session? Well, it entirely depends on the weather, the venue and the time of year. It's impossible for me to give you a definitive baiting guide for the water you're targeting without seeing each individual situation.

As a general rule, if the venue holds a good head of big carp then the 'greed factor' comes into play. If conditions were right and I thought the carp were going to feed, then I'd have no hesitation in putting a lot of bait in from the word go. In fact, at the start of this feature I introduced a gallon of maggots over one rod and topped it up every couple of hours. It worked, as I ended up with a 34lb mirror, three twenties and a couple of doubles. If you're fishing a lightly stocked water then I'd go for a completely different approach, introducing a tiny amount of bait. On a lightly stocked venue, big beds of bait can work against you. There aren't enough fish to create competition for food and as such the fish have too much bait to choose from and may end up leaving your hook bait.

Unfortunately, there are no baits that exclusively catch big carp. Believe me, I've tried everything under the sun in my quest for the ultimate big-carp bait. Red fishmeal

boilies are excellent carp bait but to be honest any bait will catch big carp on its day. Tiger nuts are another great bait and I wouldn't go carping without them. The only problem is that everybody uses these baits. As with most things in carp fishing, it pays to do something different from the norm and it's the same where bait is concerned. Maggots have been available to anglers for years and years and to this day they remain one of the best baits around. Very few carp anglers use maggots, simply because they involve a lot of messing around. They're quite fiddly to present on a rig and every fish in the lake loves maggots. However, if you stick with it, make the effort and wade through the nuisance fish, eventually the carp will move in. Very rarely will carp swim over a bed of maggots and ignore them. They absolutely adore maggots and, what's more, they're not viewed with the same suspicion as boilies and other widely used baits.

Some anglers use washed-out baits to

There are no baits that exclusively catch big carp, so be prepared.

If there are loads of carp, use loads of bait.

Glug your baits for extra attraction.

make the carp less suspicious of them. While it's not something I do, I know a few successful anglers who use this tactic. Where I'm concerned, if I have to wash out a bait to get a bite then I'd sooner change the bait I'm using altogether. In fact, I go in completely the other direction with my hook baits, opting to soak them in salmon oil or Hydro Stim. The reason behind it is attraction. The more attraction I can put into my swim to pull the carp in to investigate, the better.

When it comes down to rigs for big carp, I keep everything simple. As with bait, there is no wonder rig for catching big carp; just ensure that your rigs are strong, safe and reliable. The only difference between my big-fish rigs and my standard rigs is their length. Short rigs, between 4in and 5in, seem to be more effective at hooking big fish than long 8in to 12in hooklengths. I always test every rig I tie up before using it, dragging it across the palm of my hand to make sure that it turns in and finds a hook-hold. I'm a firm believer that, unless fishing on gravel, the lake bed will conceal your rig. The debris on the bottom is always moving and it doesn't take long for your rig to become part of the lake bed. Fishing on gravel is a different game. I always try and match the colour of my hooklength to the bottom, or use a fluorocarbon hooklength because the rig will stand out on a bed of gravel.

Unfortunately, there are no guaranteed methods, baits or features for catching big carp. But if it was that easy, would we still fish for them? At the end of the day, do your homework and fish with confidence and it'll all come good in the end.

'This NEW Bivvy Range from Prologic is packed full of features to keep you warm and dry, so you can catch those crafty carp whatever the weather!'
DEREK RITCHIE

PROLOGIC SPIDER DOME

PROLOGIC SPIDER DOME - 1 MAN & 2 MAN BIVVIES

100% Waterproof HD500 Material
Reinforced Double Stitched, Frame Sleeves
Comes Complete with stabilising bars making
it extremely rigid
Peaked Front Shelter
2 Way Door-Zip Up & Zip Down
Removable Front Door Panel Exposing
Mozzi Mesh
Roll Back Front & Side Panels
Heavy Duty, Oversized Ground Sheet
(separate to main Bivvy)
Diamond Shaped Pegging Points
Additional 'Severe Storm' Pegging Points
Wide Diameter Taped Seams
2 Internal Storage Pockets
(for mobile phone, keys etc)
Heavy Duty Zip
12 Hard Wearing Pegs Included
The 2 man dome has enough space for two
6 leg bedchairs and your luggage
Carry Bag
1 Year Manufacturers Warranty

1 MAN

ALSO AVAILABLE AS A 2 MAN

PROLOGIC SPIDER DOME

1MAN	Introductory Price	**£149.99**
2MAN	Introductory Price	**£199.99**

PROLOGIC SPIDER OVER WRAP

Wide Diameter Taped Seams
100% Waterproof HD500 Material
Cuts down the Condensation
Gives You 1/4 more ground space
Over Zip Flap-Making the zip totally
waterproof & draft proof
Diamond shaped pegging points
Clip Up Side Panels, Front door & Clear Panel
Additional 'Severe Storm' Pegging Points
Heavy duty zip
12 Hard Wearing Pegs included
Carry Bag
1 Year Manufacturers Warranty

SPIDER RANGE ALSO AVAILABLE IN MAX-4

BILL JORDAN ADVANTAGE CAMO PATTERN

MAX-4

HD HIGH DEFINITION

PRODUCED USING THE HD PROCESS

PROLOGIC SPIDER OVER WRAP

1MAN	Introductory Price	**£79.99**
2MAN	Introductory Price	**£99.99**

PROLOGIC MAX-4 SPIDER OVER WRAP

1MAN	Introductory Price	**£99.99**
2MAN	Introductory Price	**£149.99**

SVENDSEN SPORTS

CALL 029 20837981 FOR INFORMATION
ON YOUR NEAREST DEALER
www.svendsen-sports.co.uk

Mastermind

Dave Lane, one of the country's best carp anglers, answers questions on all things carpy.

Q How quickly can carp put on and lose weight? Also, would you call a carp that has been imported into the UK your UK PB?

A Around May or June, when carp approach spawning, they will drastically increase in weight, not just with spawn but also through water retention. After spawning, the weight loss is dramatic but usually short-lived as fish start to replace lost body weight through summer and autumn.

A couple of years ago I travelled out to a lake in France and, at the time, the biggest common was just over 40lb. On the first morning I had a take and landed a long, lean common of 33lb, which we weighed, photographed and returned.

Later that day we had a long conversation about the potential of the lake and the big common was mentioned many times. It was only when I arrived home and checked the photos that I realised I'd already caught it after it had shed 7lb of spawn!

On its next capture, however, it was over 42lb – so you can see how they vary from one month to the next.

In winter carp are usually fairly stable in weight and a dramatic loss between two captures could then be seen as a problem.

Another thing to take into account when comparing weights of fish is the method by which they were weighed, because everybody's results may not come out exactly the same. Some scales may be inaccurate or a mistake could have been made on one, or both, occasions.

As for an imported fish being your PB, well this is entirely up to you. There is no reason why you shouldn't class it as your biggest fish; after all, you must have been happy to fish for it in the first place.

Many fish are imported into this country and some of the most famous carp in the land have started their lives abroad. The whole subject is a very complicated one and a lot of prejudice has been born from ignorance about the implications of importing fish.

All carp were originally imported, as they are not a native species, but since then we have acquired a healthy head of carp in this country that we class as our own. But, in fact, they all have roots in other countries such as Holland, Belgium and Czechoslovakia to name but three.

Nowadays, people differentiate between recent imports and old ones (or from stock grown on) by calling them British fish and imports, but the whole picture is much more complicated than that.

The biggest fear now, and rightly so, is the importation of disease in carp; diseases that the existing stock in this country does not have an immune system against.

The most important thing is to know, when classifying imports against current stock, that they have been brought in legally and have undergone the required health checks along the way.

More recently, pressure groups like the English Carp Heritage Organisation (ECHO) have been pushing for tighter legislation and stricter health checks on imported fish, to search for new strains of virus and, hopefully, this will lead to an overall reduction of carp diseases.

This is usually a 40lb common, but lost 7lb while spawning.

Three Steps To Heaven

Jason's first thirty of the session.

Jason's oily bag mix creates a slick and will pull down cruising carp.

Jason Cann shows Marc Coulson his golden rules when targeting big carp. Follow his tips and you could be upping your personal best and catching big...

Let's get one thing straight. There is no magic formula to catching big carp. Many tackle companies might have you believe that there is a wonder rig, fail-safe set-up or even a miracle main line. There are no such things.

Equally, there is no such thing as a bait that is guaranteed to catch big carp.

I wonder how many lumps have been caught over the years on maggots, sweetcorn, worms and even bread, as well as the myriad of boilies available these days? Lots, I guess.

So, what are the golden rules when it comes to improving on your PB? How do

you go about catching that fish of a lifetime? Is it luck, are there ingredients for success or is it just a case of being in the right place at the right time?

I asked Jason Cann to shed some light on the subject. He is a man with a string of big captures to his name and is a very talented angler.

I met up with Jason at Allders Farm Fishery, not far from his home town of Milton Keynes. He'd been fishing the water on and off for the past few months in an effort to get to know the place and

ultimately bank one or two of its biggest residents.

Allders Farm boasts a decent head of carp up to mid-thirties. There are at least four over the magical 30lb barrier as well as a good number of twenties.

And here lies golden rule number one: The Right Choice Of Venue. It might sound obvious but choosing the right

Accurate casting is key when building up bait in your swim.

Jason's Jumbo Pinkie Bag

1

Pour a good handful of pinkies (like maggots but smaller) into some stocking-type PVA.

2

Jason then adds his own special bag mix. Any oily mix will do the job here.

3

Make the bags really big so that nuisance fish do not eat all the pinkies straightaway.

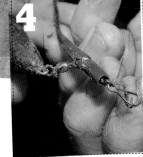

4

Jason uses a quick-change clip attached to the rig swivel in his lead clip.

5

He opens the clip, attaches the PVA bag to it and then locks it closed again.

6

The final step is to nick the hook into the bag and cast it straight out.

water is the first, and most important step in the pursuit a big carp.

"It's no good fishing a water that is stuffed full of small fish if you're after a twenty. Remember, you can only catch what is in front of you," Jason tells me. "I know there are some very big carp in here and this is why I have been fishing here for the last few months."

Jason and I had planned for him to spend some time on the venue in the hope of catching a biggie. We would then meet up to shoot some live pictures, showing how he went about targeting the carp.

He's recently caught a few Allders Farm residents up to 29lb, which is why we are here, in a bid to show how he did it.

This is his 12th visit to the water in his campaign to catch a few lumps and here lies golden rule number two: Time And Effort.

"Every week we are treated to pictures of big carp in the angling press," Jason explains. "Occasionally there is a story of a lucky angler turning up for his or her first trip to a venue and catching the biggest fish in there. This is so often the exception to the rule. The most successful anglers are those that put the time and effort into their fishing."

Jason points out that time is an important aspect of his fishing. "I am lucky enough to have time on my hands in order to go fishing. Also, especially with this venue being so close to home, I use my spare time to visit the water on non-angling trips," he said.

"I can get down here and bait up, or even just watch the water for signs of fish.

"Spending as much time as possible at the venue is key. That's not to suggest that you have to be a full-time angler in order to catch biggies.

"Even if the conditions are such that angling is out of the question, just spending a few hours watching the water might just give you a few signs.

"The more you can get to know the water the better your chances will be."

Jason is keen to stress that time away from the bank can still be used wisely.

"I have spent loads of time asking venue regulars about where the bigger fish are

You'll have to 'suffer' a few of these when fishing with pinkies.

caught. I also make sure to ask the lake owners for any catch reports before every visit."

Back to today's session and Jason demonstrates one of the essentials, location. Having originally ditched our gear in a swim at the shallow end of the lake, Jason takes a wander back to the hut to check on a few things.

He returns and beckons me to start moving the tackle to the deeper, dam-wall end of the lake. Apparently, the last two carp, both twenties, had been caught from this end of the lake and so it is a natural starting point for today.

The moment we turn and head towards the dam, a big carp leaps clear of the water and lands back down, no more than a yard off the dam wall, with a huge 'spadoosh'!

"This proves the point about observing the water. There are no prizes for guessing where the first rod is going!" Jason laughs. So what about Jason's tactics for today? While we

Bloody hell, it's heavy.

The rig that accounted for Jason's seond thirty of the session.

A baiting spoon makes feeding maggots and pinkies easy.

are here to get some pictures of the tactics he used to catch those twenties, including the 29-pounder, Jason is keen to get the rods out in an effort to catch a lump for the cameras.

"You never know, I might even tempt one of the thirties," he quips.

You might be forgiven for thinking that, in order to catch a big carp, Jason is using big baits. However, you would be wrong, very wrong.

He produces a bucket of what appears to be maggots. I am a little surprised at first but then he tells me they are actually pinkies – an even smaller bait.

"There are a lot of anglers that target this venue with boilies and I want to do something different," says Jason. "There are lots of silver fish – roach, rudd and even bream - in here and I want to cause some commotion by attracting these fish first."

This brings us to Jason's final golden rule: Patience. From the moment that Jason's first PVA bag of pinkies hits the lake bed, his buzzers constantly bleep to signal the presence of these 'nuisance' fish.

"I am hoping that all the commotion from the small fish, as well as the rising oils from my bag mix, will cause any cruising carp to investigate.

"It's all about being patient and wading through some smaller fish."

Jason is proved right as, after unhooking three roach in succession, one of his rods roars off.

"This is no roach," he cries as he picks his rod up.

Sure enough, the culprit is a small

common of around a pound. However, this does not put Jason off.

"The very fact that there are big carp in here means that the next carp to come along could be one of those lumps," he says.

Jason's rod rips off again and we both know what's coming!

"This is a proper one, mate," Jason shouts as he struggles to stay in touch with the fish.

Jason slowly manages to gain line and eventually has the fish in the margin. As it breaks the surface Jason declares that it is indeed one of the big fish and we both fancy it could even be one of the thirties.

He guides the huge carp into the net and punches the air in delight. What better way to highlight his big-fish tactics than

The '29' that Jason caught a few months before, but this time at 30lb 1oz.

with a carp such as this?

Neither myself nor Jason are surprised when the dial of his scales settles on 31lb 10oz. What a result! We take a few pictures before Jason slips it back into the lake.

As we sit back down I notice the water rocking in the near margin before a huge bow wave streams out across the entire lake.

In a flash, Jason drops a baited rig on the spot, this time with a bright boilie on the hook.

Within 10 minutes the margin rod pulls violently round. After another frantic battle Jason nets another huge Allders Farm carp. As he lifts up the landing net Jason recognises the carp as the '29' that he caught a few weeks back.

Not to be greedy, we agree that a thirty and an upper twenty is a right result. However, the day gets even better when the scales reveal that this carp has been feeding and, at 30lb 1oz, it is the icing on today's cake.

So, there you go. The secret to catching big carp does not lie in some mystical bait or wonder rig but instead in the location, the effort you put in and the ability to bide your time.